The Philosophy of Humour

—

PHILOSOPHY INSIGHTS

GENERAL EDITOR: MARK ADDIS

The Philosophy of Humour

Paul McDonald

$\mathcal{HEB}$ ☼ Humanities-Ebooks

COPYRIGHT

This edition published by *Humanities-Ebooks, LLP,* Tirril Hall, Tirril, Penrith CA10 2JE

ISBN 978-1-84760-210-7 PDF
ISBN 978-1-84760-212-1 Kindle
ISBN 978-1-84760-238-1 Paperback

Contents

Acknowledgments

I'd like to thank Professor Mark Addis whose excellent suggestions influenced the final shape of this volume. I'd also like to thank my two fellow humour enthusiasts at the University of Wolverhampton, Josiane Boutonnet and Jackie Pieterick, with whom I have had many enjoyable discussions about humour, and who have influenced my thinking on the subject markedly.

1. Introduction

The American philosopher Ted Cohen refuses to offer a universal theory of joking because he doesn't think such a thing exists. Certainly there are numerous competing theories of humour and laughter, and the quest to adequately theorise them is as old as philosophy itself. The absence of a single theory implies the importance of assessing the various competing theories, of course, and one aim of this book is to do exactly that.

Humour has been discussed from a host of different perspectives over the years, many of which fall outside the discipline of philosophy. While concentrating chiefly on philosophical approaches to humour, this discussion inevitably moves into other fields such as cultural studies, literary theory, religion, psychoanalysis, and psychology; the broad focus will hopefully make for a richer account of humour and its bearing on the human condition.

Humour is a creative activity, and another aim of this book is to address that aspect of humour. Research shows that people are more receptive to new concepts when they are in a 'humorous mode,' and they are also more creative. Throughout the book readers will be invited to engage in creative writing exercises designed to exploit this crucial facet of humour, and to help them explore relevant issues imaginatively. In this way they will deepen their understanding of those issues, whilst at the same time cultivating their own creative skills. Thus the book will be of value both to people interested in the meaning of humour, and to those wishing to explore its creative possibilities. Students of philosophy will find the creative writing exercises useful in helping to engage with the debates that surround humour, whilst creative writers will discover that thinking philosophically about humour can lead to a better appreciation of how it might work for them in their creative lives. Also, at various points throughout the book, readers will be invited to 'pause and reflect' on key issues; again this is intended to encourage active engagement with the topics under the discussion.

1.1 Humour or Laughter?

Pause and Reflect

What is the difference between laughter and humour? How are they related?

The title of this book refers to humour, and it is worth saying something about what this means, and how the word has signified through history. It has its origins in the Latin *umor*, which meant liquid. In medieval medicine it referred specifically to the liquids that were thought to comprise people, and which need to be in proportion if one is to be healthy. There were four: blood, phlegm, yellow bile, and black bile. Too much blood made people sanguine and over–excited, too much phlegm made them phlegmatic and sluggish, excess yellow bile made them choleric and irritable, while too much black bile caused melancholy, anger and depression. Only with all four fluids in balance were people deemed healthy, and in good humour; attempting to make people feel better came to be known as humouring them. This in turn led to the term being used to indicate a person's state of mind, with the first evidence of this appearing in the sixteenth century when 'good humour' began to denote cheerfulness. Later one of its connotations was eccentricity, or behaviour incompatible with social norms, and it is this sense of the word that underpins its associations with the comic; by the eighteenth century it denoted funniness and the state of being amused. Laughter can have negative associations, and in the eighteenth century humanist philosophers began to use the word humour to distinguish acceptable forms of laughter and amusement from morally dubious forms like sarcasm, mockery, and wit, which were thought to demean people. The term humour was reserved for benign and non–aggressive amusement. As a result a 'sense of humour' came to be seen as something worth cultivating, and by the nineteenth century having a capacity for humour was deemed a virtue. In the modern world the word has lost this specific meaning, however, and tends to be used as a general synonym for joking, comedy and laughter.

So over the centuries humour meant different things, and the philosophers of the ancient world did not use the word at all. Their focus is mostly on laughter. Indeed, throughout this book there is much reference to laughter, and it is worth noting that there is an essential distinction to be made between humour and laughter. Obviously they are often related, but not always. Laughter is a physical activity that can exist without humour; the source of laughter doesn't have to be comic and can result from being tickled, from inhaling laughing gas, from nervousness, from a shock, or from other non–humorous stimuli. Similarly, not all instances of humour generate laughter. For one thing, people need to find things funny before they'll laugh, and what counts as humour for one person won't necessarily work for another. It is perfectly possible to discern humorous intent in something without actually finding it funny enough to laugh at. There are lots of different kinds of humour, and some of the subtler forms may not produce physical laughter as such. Here the word amusement is useful, and some modern philosophers actually prefer this to humour. It can denote a humorous state of mind in which laughter may be absent, while the word humour itself can be reserved specifically for referring to objects of amusement. However, not all are so precise with their language, and often, particularly in twentieth century philosophy and humour theory, the terms humour, laughter, joking, comedy, amusement, mirth, etc., are used synonymously. As this book deals with a variety of approaches to humour, I will use terms as they are employed by the philosophers in question, while in general discussions I will use whichever term is most appropriate in context.

Creative Writing Exercise

Create a funny scene in which a comic novelist and a stand-up comedian argue about the relationship between humour and laughter, and the importance of the connection between the two. Try to use as many synonyms for humour and laughter as possible in the dialogue, and think about which character might use which terms, and why.

It is useful to do this exercise, and indeed most of the exercises in the book, with interested friends because this creates a mutual audience: someone else's laughter always has the potential to stimulate you to higher levels of comic creativity. As will be seen, depending on which philosophy of humour you subscribe to, there are various reasons why this might be the case.

2. The Origins and Evolution of Humour

2.1 The Emergence of Humour

No society has ever been discovered that doesn't use humour, and it seems to have been around for tens of thousands of years. When Australian aboriginals were first encountered by westerners it was noted that they could perceive and generate humour. As they had been isolated genetically for a minimum of 35,000 years, it probably follows that humour is at least as old as this.[1] It has also been part our cultural life from the beginning. Humour occurs in some of the oldest texts in existence, such as those written in cuneiform in ancient Sumer up to five thousand years ago. Many Sumerian riddles and proverbs clearly have a humorous dimension, and some Sumerian tales have structures akin to those found in modern jokes, such as the riddle form and the 'rule of three.' Likewise, humour was very much a part of life in ancient Egypt, where it features in their narratives and artworks, and in ancient Greece where professional jokers could make a living as entertainers.

The consensus is that humour is an exclusively human activity. While many mammals exhibit bared–teeth displays akin to laughter, most agree that only humans have the requisite cognitive capability to create humour. It seems certain that an ability to appreciate incongruity is important for humour, and it is thought that human beings began to develop this—or at least an ability to juxtapose disparate concepts—roughly 50,000 years ago. One early example of this development is the Lion Man figure found in 1939 in the Swabian Alps, Germany and thought to be about 35,000 years old. Carved from a mammoth's tusk, the figure has the body of a lion and the legs of a man; this

1 See Joseph Polimeni and Jeffrey P. Reiss, 'The First Joke: Exploring the Evolutionary Origins of Humor,' *Evolutionary Psychology*, Volume 1, 2006, 347–366 (347).

yoking together of man and animal creates the kind of mismatch or contradiction that is often present in humour. Interestingly it has been suggested that humanity's capacity for spiritual thought emerged around the same time, and that this may be related to our ability to entertain humour. Humour and spiritual thought both demonstrate thinking that allows what Joseph Polimeni and Jeffrey P. Reiss refer to as 'a direct violation of an ontological category;' ('The First Joke,' 360–361); in other words, this level of thought permits one distinct plane of being or existence to be entertained simultaneously with another: human and animal in the case of the Lion Man; natural and supernatural in the case of spiritual thought. For an example of how this relates to humour consider the following joke:

> What happened to the Pope when he went to Mount Olive?
> Popeye beat him up.[2]

Here the world of twentieth century cartoons is juxtaposed with a figure from reality, and to fully appreciate the joke you need to recognise the difference between these categories, and hence the 'violation' at work in the narrative. While this joke contrasts ontological classifications in an obvious way (to make the point), clearly not all humour does so, but combinations of disparate elements are almost always part of humour, and an ability to perceive them seems to be fundamental.

No one knows for certain why or how humour developed in humans, and there is probably more than one reason, but some clues may be found in the relationship between humour and play. The work of ethnologists like Jan van Hoof show that primates exhibit facial expressions akin to human laughter when they're signalling that they are in play mode and their behaviour should not be taken seriously. Likewise, babies and toddlers laugh and smile in similar situations to those where primates show play mode expressions. As children's cognitive skills develop, so does the sophistication of their play, and their ability to use humour as a part of that play; as they grow, so their humorous play becomes more abstract and cerebral. Early human's

---

2   Unless otherwise stated all of the jokes used in this book are in the public domain. For a list of sources for jokes, see the 'online material' section of the Bibliography.

capacity to use humour may have developed in a similar way, as their cognitive capacity evolved. John Morreall, for instance, suggests that, 'For early humans to develop humour [...] they had to acquire this ability to play with thoughts.'[3] Thus humour seems to be linked to an ability and desire to relocate play in the mind; a capability— that animals don't have—to utilise our creative faculties in order to achieve the pleasure of play in a cerebral context.

Pause and Reflect

Think of some of the ways our ancestors may have benefitted from humour; clues might be found in how humour features in modern life.

2.2 The Benefits of Humour

Darwin said that there must be some sort of evolutionary advantage associated with humour, and it does indeed appear that humans developed it directly because it has numerous positive properties, and very few negative ones. Laughing uses up energy, perhaps, and the noise created by laughter might have made our early ancestors vulnerable to predators, but these potential problems are far outweighed by the benefits. Some argue that the pleasure associated with humorous exchange replaced the pleasure derived from social grooming at some stage in our development: both 'laughter and social grooming release endogenous opiates' and so 'the feelings of gratification positively reinforce' both types of behaviour. Thus it seems that one early function of humour was as a social lubricant, and 'the fundamental evolutionary purpose of humour and laughter was to facilitate cooperation between people;' essentially, 'a laughing response signals that one is both ready and able to cooperate' (Joseph Polimeni and Jeffrey P. Reiss, 'The First Joke,' 352). Observations of primates suggest that humour might be linked to our need to partake of mock–aggression and create safe spaces where social conflicts can be resolved; similarly anthropologists note that humour in traditional societies often

---

3   John Morreall, *A Comprehensive Philosophy of Humor* (Chichester: John Wiley & Sons, 2009) 43.

takes the form of joking relationships between people, or individual clowning whose purpose is to avoid or assuage tensions. Humour can enable expressions of pseudo–violence, mock sexual overtures, and activities that allow the saving of face; it permits social hierarchies to be sustained, and can work to reinforce social bonds.

Evolutionary theorists like R.D. Alexander argue that humour could have helped to increase an individual's success at mating, boosting their status in relation to others; in this way it again potentially facilitates social bonding, enhancing the social status of those who share a joke at the expense of the butt of the joking, and thus increasing unity among the 'in' group. It is easy to see this function of humour at work in modern society of course. The ability to use humour is still a route to popularity in most cultures, and 'in' group individuals are commonly more attractive to the opposite sex. V.S. Ramachandran, meanwhile, argues that laughter may have developed as a signal that something which at first appears dangerous is actually safe: 'the main purpose of laughter is for the individual to alert others in the social group that the anomaly detected by that individual is of trivial consequence' (see Polimeni and Reiss, 'The First Joke,' 351–2). This 'false alarm theory' implies that humour in early human societies worked to lessen fears about ostensibly threatening differences between group members. Again this experience is a familiar one in the modern world; laughter is often the result when an apparently frightening situation turns out to be benign.

It may well be that humour has helped with the development of our cognitive and creative faculties too. Jonathan Miller, for instance, contends that the 'biological payoff' for an ability to use humour might have:

> something to do with the exercise of some sort of perception which enables us to see things for the first time, to reconsider our categories and therefore to be a little more flexible and versatile when we come to deal with the world in the future [...] The more we laugh the more we see the point of things, the better we are, the cleverer we are at reconsidering what the world is like. [We use] the experience of humour as sabbatical leave from the binding categories that we use as rules

of thumb to allow us to conduct our way around the world. This is why humour plays such an important part in our social arrangements.[4]

Miller sees humour as an arena where norms—'binding categories'—can be dodged, which may lead to new insights and aid creative thinking. Humour allows us to free ourselves from conventional patterns of thought and create a place where we can interrogate those patterns, and entertain alternatives to them. In this respect humour has enormous creative potential. For artists it is crucial to escape the 'binding categories' of everyday life, such as the clichés we inherit and which we should jettison if our thinking is to be anything other than banal.

Creative Writing Exercise

Take a day off from banality and try the following exercise. Imagine a scene in which a character is facing a firing squad. His executers agree to spare the condemned man if he can come up with a non–clichéd, amusing euphemism for 'kick the bucket' in exactly five minutes. Describe his thoughts, and the various alternative metaphors and similes that occur to him at this moment of crisis; try to make them as amusing as possible in an effort to escape those 'binding categories' that Miller mentions.

2.3 Is Humour an Emotion?

Throughout the centuries many philosophers have treated humour as an emotion, but not all agree that this is the case. A discussion of the origins of humour is a good place to consider this issue because, as will be seen, it has some bearing on how and why humour might have developed.

Pause and Reflect

Does humour differ from the things we call emotions: for example, love, hate, fear, joy, jealousy, sadness? Are there ways in which

---

4 Quoted in Jerry Palmer, *Taking Humour Seriously* (London: Routledge, 1994) 57–8.

humour might relate to these emotions?

The Case For

Let's begin with the view that humour qualifies as an emotion. The British philosopher Robert Sharpe (1935–2006), for instance, is of the opinion that it is an emotion, and he offers no less than seven reasons why he thinks so.[5] Preferring the term amusement to humour, he argues that amusement is like other emotions in that it has an object. Just as one might love or hate some object or other, so an object is a necessary stimulus for amusement. Also there are degrees of amusement, just as there are degrees of other emotions; for example, just as it's possible for the emotion of fear to range from a little scared to absolutely terrified, so it is possible to be mildly amused by something at one extreme, or reduced to paroxysms of laughter at the other. Another parallel is that, as with emotions, we can only partially supress or stifle amusement. It is often easy to tell when someone is trying to conceal fear, for instance, by the physical signals they cannot master; likewise there are various uncontrollable physical signs that can betray amusement. Most people will identify with this if they've been in situations where laughter is inappropriate, but impossible to quash. Also amusement, like emotions, can be the cause of self–deception. Just as we might not want to admit fear, for instance, so we might be reluctant to admit amusement; we know we shouldn't laugh at politically incorrect jokes, for example, and may be inclined to conceal the fact that we do. Emotions tend to be either positive or negative too: love is positive, hate is negative, and so on; amusement is generally thought to be a positive experience. Another similarity, according to Sharpe, is the distinction between 'cause and object' that is common to emotions. So while death might be the object of fear, it can't be the cause of fear because it has not occurred. Similar distinctions can be observed in examples of amusement. It is possible, for instance, to laugh at the punch line of a joke before it is delivered, just as it is possible to laugh at someone's anticipated reac-

---

5 Robert Sharpe, 'Seven Reasons Why Amusement is an Emotion,' in John Morreall., ed., *The Philosophy of Laughter and Humor* (New York: State University of New York Press) 208–211 (209).

tion to it; here then is a distinction between the cause and the object of amusement which would seem to qualify it as an emotion.

One apparent objection to categorising amusement as an emotion has to do with the similarities between amusement and aesthetic appreciation. In other words amusement is a matter of taste, and taste can be cultivated in ways that emotions cannot. We can learn to appreciate humour, just as we can learn to appreciate various art forms; also, like our appreciation of art objects, our taste in amusement 'progresses towards the more subtle forms;' and as our appreciation of amusement develops so it can become more complex and sophisticated (hence critical terms like corny and clichéd apply as much to humour as they do to art). At first sight this seems to preclude its status as an emotion: as Sharpe points out, we cannot imagine cultivating a taste in jealousy or fear as we tend not to have that kind of control over emotions. Sharpe gets around this, however, by arguing that some emotions are indeed 'susceptible to cultivation;' significantly these are the emotions that tend to constitute responses to art: 'I can cultivate a love for the novels of Conrad [for instance] I nurture this affection by rereading and extending my knowledge of Conrad and so on' (Robert Sharpe, 'Seven Reasons Why Amusement is an Emotion,' 211). In other words, emotions such as love *can* be a matter of taste, and these, like amusement, can be nurtured and developed.

The Case Against

The case against thinking of humour as an emotion is argued cogently by John Morreall. Again he prefers the term amusement, and he makes the point that our capacity to be amused takes place at a sophisticated level, demanding a high degree of cognitive development. For Morreall amusement depends on our ability to enjoy having our expectations about the world violated, and this requires a different kind of thinking to that associated with emotions. More importantly, emotions have a practical dimension that amusement does not:

An emotion involves our practical concern, usually with our

current situation or that of someone to whom we are attached [...] Amusement, by contrast, involves a non–practical attitude toward some present or non–present (often even non–real) situation that need have no relation at all to us.[6]

Emotions developed in order to enable humans to deal with practical situations: fear was our signal of danger, anger our signal to fight, and so on. While there are higher emotions that might at first seem to have no practical application, these are invariably linked to those more basic emotions that *do* have practical purposes. So, for instance, emotions such as resentment and indignation are higher order emotions which have their roots in anger; and even in their higher state retain a practical facet, 'in that they are a response to something harmful done to or by a person, and in that they serve as negative reinforcement for the one perpetuating the harm not to repeat the action' (John Morreall, 'Humor and Emotion,' 219–20). Amusement differs because it does not have a practical purpose of this kind, nor is it linked to a more basic emotion that does. In fact, importantly, there is a sense in which practical emotions and amusement are at odds with one another. When amusement *does* become associated with an emotion, the latter can undermine the former: the practical concern that the emotion evokes can eclipse the amusement. We are less likely to find someone amusing when we are furious with them, for instance; or at the other extreme, when we are engaged in a passionate sexual encounter with them. Morreall believes that we may have developed a capacity for amusement alongside our capacity for reason, and humour may have assisted in the development of reason precisely because of its ability to block emotions:

> for emotions, which served pre–human animals so well, would often get in the way of rational thinking, as indeed they still do. To be able to face incongruity in one's experience—especially one's own failure—with amusement instead of anger or sadness, allows a person a more objective and rational perspective on what is happening (John Morreall, 'Humor and

---

6　John Morreall, 'Humor and Emotion,' in John Morreall., ed., *The Philosophy of Laughter and Humor* (New York: State University of New York Press, 1987) 212–224 (217).

Emotion,' 223).

When we are in a humorous mode we are not practical, we are play-ful, and this playful state of mind can give us a valuable perspec-tive on our lives, without which we would be incapable of reason. So amusement is antithetical to the emotions in this respect; while emotions encroach on and retard rational thinking, amusement ena-bles it, offering the possibility of detachment from the more practi-cally oriented emotions. Of course it is possible for this detachment to be negative, particularly when we use humour to avoid emotional engagement. Humour can be employed callously in this way, particu-larly as a response to human suffering. In his book, *Engaging Humor* (2003), for instance, Elliott Oring argues that humour has been used as a means of supressing sentiment in America; humour takes the place of sentimental expression which came to be devalued in the nineteenth century.[7] You have probably noticed in your own life that some find it easier to make a joke than to show emotion. The ability for humour to work in this way explains the existence of so-called gallows humour, the term used to describe the tendency toward dark humour found among people who work in professions that confront death on a daily basis.

Creative Writing Exercise

Humour can be used to good effect in writing because of its capacity to offset excessive emotion. Disproportionate sentimentality, for instance, is viewed negatively in the arts, and whenever writing is in danger of becoming oversentimental humour can provide a valuable corrective. With this in mind, create a scene in which an old man is dying in a hospital bed surrounded by his family. Can you think of any ways in which you can bring humour to the scene? Try experimenting with dialogue, the interior thoughts of his family, potential intrusions from other characters (medical staff, etc.), the physical surroundings, and so on. Notice how humour can change the patina and import of the scene.

---

7 Elliott Oring, *Engaging Humor* (University of Illinois Press, 2003) see chapter 6.

3. The Earliest Philosophies of Humour

3.1 Plato

Though the Pre–Socratic philosopher Democritus (460–370 BC) was known as the 'laughing philosopher', apparently because he had a humorous nature and enjoyed mocking his peers, he didn't write much of significance about laughter. Plato (428–348 BC) is the first philosopher to comment substantially on comedy and laughter, although his focus is chiefly on the latter. Plato didn't much approve of laughter because he felt that it was allied to base instincts that are at odds with reason. His *Republic* (380 BC) debates the relationship between the ideal person and the ideal state, and whenever laughter is addressed it is as something that may threaten the ideal. For Plato the causes of laughter are exterior to the individual, something that infect us from without and which upset our serious nature; in the *Republic* reason is celebrated above everything and counters the disruptive urge to partake of laughter: the ideal state of the individual is serious, in other words, and feelings that threaten to undermine that seriousness—such as laughter—should be kept in check:

> There's a part of you which wants to make people laugh, but your reason restrains it, because you're afraid of being thought a vulgar clown. Nevertheless you let it have its own way on those other occasions, and you don't realize that the almost inevitable result of giving it energy in this other context is that you become a comedian in your own life.[8]

For Plato the comedian, or 'buffoon,' is an unruly force, at odds with the cultivation of dignity.

8　Plato, *Republic*, X, trans., Robin Waterfield (Oxford: Oxford University Press, 1993) 360.

The *Republic* goes on to draw parallels between clowning and those emotions related to sex and anger, which should also be managed for the sake of a 'better' and 'happier' life. It's proposed that the Guardians of Plato's ideal state must avoid laughter lest they become prone to its destructive possibilities. To ensure that this doesn't happen, Plato felt that their education should be purged of any references to heroes or gods laughing uncontrollably: only serious role models are suitable for the occupants of this important job.

Plato deals with laughter more substantially in the *Philebus* (360–347 BC), which takes the form of dialogues between Philebus, Socrates, and Protarchus. Here the theme is the contrast between a life of pleasure and a life of intelligence: Philebus—whose name means 'loverboy'—argues in favour of pleasure, while Socrates argues for a life of the mind. Protarchus, meanwhile, disparages laughter because he feels that it's associated with malice. When we laugh at a friend's misfortune we feel pleasure, and malice is the source of that pleasure; Plato underscores this by putting the following words into the mouth of Socrates:

> Then our argument shows that when we laugh at what is ridiculous in our friends, our pleasure, in mixing with malice, mixes with pain, for we have agreed that malice is a pain of the soul, and that laughter is pleasant, and on these occasions we both feel malice and laugh.[9]

Plato sees such laughter as a bad thing certainly, and the fact that it is associated with pleasure suggests that it's something we are drawn to, against our better judgement. It seems odd that the pleasure of laughter isn't seen as positive, but we need to remember that for Plato such pleasures have the potential to corrupt one's judgment. Yet there is some ambivalence in his view that, while laughing at a friend's misfortune is wrong and should be avoided, there is nothing wrong with laughing at our enemies.

In *Laws* (360 BC), Plato argues that witnessing a comic performance on stage can be good for an audience because, as S.H. Butcher writes:

---

9   Plato, *Philebus*, 48-50, trans. Benjamin Jowett (Project Gutenberg EBook #1744) unpaginated.

It may serve an educational end; for the serious implies the ludicrous, and opposites cannot be understood without opposites. The citizens, therefore, may witness the representation of comedy on the stage in order to avoid doing what is ludicrous in life; but only under the proviso that the characters shall not be acted except by slaves.[10]

This suggests that the comic can have a constructive social function in the sense that it offers an example against errant behaviour—we will see that this view crops up often in theories of humour. Plato also acknowledges the possibility of making serious points through comedy, and touches on the notion that is it possible for comic expression to become a vehicle for unpalatable truths. Plato doesn't really develop this, however, and despite acknowledging the beneficial possibilities of a comic performance, he fails to fully explore any potentially positive aspects of comedy or laughter. Indeed, elsewhere in *Laws* Plato again disparages laughter, particularly when it is aimed at an individual, because 'there is no man who is in the habit of laughter at another who does not miss virtue and earnestness altogether, or lose the better half of greatness.'[11]

One important thing to note is the relationship Plato sees between laughter and superiority. In his view laughter is created as a result of other people's state of being 'ridiculous' compared to ourselves, and situations in which laughter occur are invariably hierarchical; clearly this corresponds to our contemporary sense of there being a 'butt' of a joke. In this respect Plato's reading of laughter has had an influence on Superiority Theory, an important theory of comedy and laughter that will be discussed in detail later.

Despite his largely negative views, there could be said to be humour of sorts at work in some of Plato's own writing. In his dialogues he presents Socrates as a figure adept at irony: in one sense Socrates can be seen as a genius who acts dumb as a strategy for disarming people in order to educate them. Plato calls him the *eiron*: an ostensibly

10 S.H. Butcher, *Aristotle's Theory of Poetry and Fine Art* (New York: Dover, 1951) 205.

11 Plato, *Laws*. Book 11, trans. Benjamin Jowett (Project Gutenberg EBook #1750), unpaginated.

self–deprecating individual who pretends to be ignorant, despite being knowledgeable and highly intelligent. Irony can be a form of humour, and while Socrates never laughs, this use of irony casts him is something of a trickster; a joker. Consider the following dialogue, which is a variation of a well–known modern joke at the expense of Socrates:

> **Dumb Dave**: Hey Socrates, guess what I just heard about one of your students.
>
> **Socrates**: Hold on. Before you tell me, I'd like to subject it to the Triple Filter Test
>
> **Dumb Dave**: Wha?
>
> **Socrates**: Before you talk to me about my student let's take a moment to filter what you're going to say, to see if it's worthy of consideration. The first filter is Truth. Have you made absolutely sure that what you are about to tell me is true?
>
> **Dumb Dave**: I'm not expert on truth, but I'd have to say no: I only just heard about it.
>
> **Socrates**: So you don't really know if it's true or not. Now let's try the second filter, the filter of Goodness. Is what you are about to tell me about my student something good?
>
> **Dumb Dave**: I'm no expert on ethics, but I'd say it's the opposite of good.
>
> **Socrates**: So you want to tell me something bad about him, even though you're not certain it's true?
>
> **Dumb Dave**: Er, yep.
>
> **Socrates**: This isn't encouraging, but there is a third filter: the filter of Usefulness. Is what you want to tell me about my student going to be useful to me?
>
> **Dumb Dave**: I'm no expert on value, but I'd say no.
>
> **Socrates**: If it is neither true, good, nor useful, then perhaps you should keep it to yourself.
>
> **Dumb Dave**: You know best Socrates.
>
> **Moral**: This dialogue demonstrates why Socrates was a great philosopher and held in such high esteem. It also explains why he never found out that Plato was screwing his wife.

Here you could say that Socratic irony is turned against the master: the joke constructs Socrates as a know–all, and Dumb Dave's apparent dumbness exposes the shortcomings of the so–called 'triple theory test.' Assuming that Dumb Dave isn't really dumb, then the line 'You know best Socrates' is clearly ironic.

Not only is irony an important facet of humour, but it has also been a significant tool for philosophers and other intellectuals over the years; for instance, during times of oppression when ideas must be hinted at rather than expressed outright, then ambivalent, ironic language can be invaluable. Humour's ability to simultaneously say things and not say them—in other words its ability to be 'only joking'—gives it incredible potential as a safe mode of communication.

Creative Writing Exercise

Try to create a dialogue in which one of the speakers becomes the victim of another's irony. Make sure that whoever reads the dialogue can pick up on the irony. The joke above ensures this in a very crude way by including a moral at the end. Remember, irony is present when the ostensible meaning is at odds with the real meaning. When trying to create irony in writing it is always worth reflecting on how that real meaning is being signalled to the reader. Irony, like humour in general, tends to be in the eye of the beholder: if they don't see it, it isn't there.

3.2 Aristotle

Aristotle (348–322) agrees with Plato that laughter is often associated with immoderate behaviour, and he acknowledges the element of superiority and malice that is frequently present; like Plato he is suspicious of it. However, for Aristotle the pleasure to be had from the 'ludicrous' is not just about another person's misfortune. Indeed, Aristotle recognises a version of the ludicrous that doesn't necessarily occasion derisive laughter. In his book on narrative theory, *Poetics* (350 BC), he talks extensively about comedy, and says the following:

Comedy is, as we have said, an imitation of characters of a lower type—not, however, in the full sense of the word bad, the ludicrous being merely a subdivision of the ugly. It consists in some defect or ugliness which is not painful or destructive. To take an obvious example, the comic mask is ugly and distorted, but does not imply pain.[12]

The comic mask is not associated with human distress or with anything necessarily destructive: it suggests a painless distortion. This seems to allow the possibility of a more benign laughter. Indeed, S.H. Butcher argues, that Aristotle's notion of 'ugly' can be extended to include 'the frailties, follies, and infirmities of human nature, as distinguished from its graver vices or crimes;' in fact Butcher feels that it can be extended even further to include 'the incongruities, absurdities, or cross–purposes of life, its blunders and discords, its imperfect correspondences and adjustments.'(Butcher, *Aristotle's Theory,* 375). If we accept this then the source of laughter becomes something other than malice or superiority. It raises the question of whether it's possible for such 'incongruities' to create humour in and of themselves: can humans be amused simply as a result of perceiving such absurdities, regardless of another's misfortune or inferiority? Some, like Butcher, feel that Aristotle's views on comedy anticipate Incongruity Theory which, as will be seen later, is an important theory that sees humour as something created by mismatched juxtapositions and contradictions. When talking of dramatic comedy, for instance, Aristotle suggests that laughter is often created when an audience's expectations are undermined, and he offers this example from a Greek drama: 'as he walked, beneath his feet were—chilblains.'[13] Here we are expecting a word like sandals, but we get chilblains instead; in other words there is an incongruity between our expectation and reality. Arguably there need be no malice associated with the laughter produced by such painless contrasts.

While he does not approve of comedy that attacks individuals or named personalities, Aristotle praises comic works that address universal themes and gently satirise human folly. For this reason he had more time for writers like the Greek dramatist Menander (342–

---

12 Aristotle, *Poetics.* In S.H. Butcher, trans., *Aristotle's Theory of Poetry and Fine Art* (New York: Dover, 1951) 21.

13 In the *Rhetoric,* 3.2, quoted in John Morreall, 'The Rejection of Humor in Western Thought,' *Philosophy East & West* V. 39 No. 3 (July 1989) 243-265 (248).

291 BC), than for those like Aristophanes who savagely caricatured historical figures. In the *Nicomachean Ethics* Aristotle also has positive things to say about people who use humour in a 'tactful' way, and whom he refers to as 'witty.' He contrasts such people with those who take joking too far, and who pursue it even when it's plainly upsetting for the butt of the joke; such people he calls 'vulgar buffoons.'

Pause and Reflect

Is the issue of excess relevant to humour? Think about ways in which it might be possible to overdo comedy.

Nicomachean Ethics is Aristotle's best known work on ethics and it deals with how best to attain happiness and a good life. The route to happiness is via the cultivation of necessary virtues, and for Aristotle virtue is associated with moderation: an adherence to the principle of balance or 'the middle state.' Wit, along with amiability and sincerity is one of the three social virtues, but as with other human activities it is desirable only in moderation. While the witty, tactful man who cultivates moderation is fine, those who get carried away with their clowning must be viewed negatively. The buffoon is one such person for Aristotle; this type will say things that respectable people would not, and lacks control and sensitivity when joking. Adhering to the mean requires restraint, and restraint is difficult when laughter is around; as with Plato, laughter is a potentially corrupting force for Aristotle: he thought that most people are inclined to go over the top with their joking and habitually over-indulge at the expense of more edifying pursuits. In short people should refrain from joking excessively, and some subjects, such as the law, or jokes about individuals are out of bounds.

While the buffoon becomes corrupted by laughter, Aristotle feels that moderate joking can have a moral dimension: the person who exhibits restrained wit can become a model of correct behaviour; in this respect his views create a foundation for much subsequent thinking about humour, as Barry Sanders argues:

Aristotle makes an astounding claim: While the buffoon is turned into a slave of laughter, the true wit stands solidly as a free person and from that position can legislate against others! Of all things, laughter can liberate and lift a person into a new category—the democratic, free soul. Thus situated, one can face the world as a free spirited leader who commands respect from others—all because of one's correct attitude toward laughter. This is a most important contribution to the history of the laughable, for Aristotle's distinction between the liberal and the illiberal jest will be used to rationalize joking into the Roman period, and well beyond into Cicero's time.[14]

So like Plato, Aristotle is wary of laughter, but he can appreciate the power and the possibilities of the comic: if we cultivate the 'correct attitude toward laughter' it is potentially liberating and ennobling, and the individual who can use comedy appropriately is in possession of a valuable skill indeed.

3.3 Cicero

'If you're going to tell people the truth, be funny or they'll kill you.' —Billy Wilder.

Someone else who was aware of how valuable wit and joking can be is the Roman philosopher and statesman, Cicero (106–43 BC). He discusses comedy and laughter in *De Oratore* (*On the Orator*), where he describes the perfect orator and the techniques required for persuasive speaking. Many scholars have speculated about whether this text may have been directly influenced by Aristotle. That influence might have come via a treatise on humour called *Tractatus Coislinianus*, which some think contains a summary of Aristotle's views on comedy as expressed in the lost second volume of *Poetics*. Though its existence is debateable, it's possible that this second volume expanded Aristotle's views on comedy. Certainly *Tractatus Coislinianus* does appear to bear the mark of Aristotle's thinking,

---

14 Barry Sanders, *Sudden Glory: Laughter as Subversive History* (Boston: Beacon Press, 1995) 106–7.

particularly in its suggestion that comedy, like tragedy, can result in catharsis—a kind of purgation or purification of the emotions. This work also suggests that laughter can be created either by the things people say, or the things they do, a distinction also found in Cicero's thinking, as we'll see. There is no way of proving that Cicero read *Tractatus Coislinianus*, although he does admit to consulting several treaties on humour and it seems likely that this was one of them.[15] Like Aristotle, Cicero notes that laughter can be associated with deformity and low behaviour, and he also agrees that one needs to be selective about topics for joking, and wary of how far it should go; he insists that people's feelings should always be taken into account. Cicero also followed Aristotle in identifying incongruity as a feature of comedy, noticing that most jokes lead us to expect something only to qualify that expectation: in his view it is the disappointment at having an expectation undermined that creates laughter.

Pause and Reflect

Most people would agree that an ability to be funny is often desirable when it comes to public speaking; why do you think that is? Also, you occasionally hear people speak about 'truth' being revealed through humour. In what sense might this be possible?

For Cicero comedy is a gift from the gods, and it is a positive force for the orator partly because of its capacity to offset solemnity, and even ameliorate potential offense. In Cicero's words 'it mitigates and relaxes gravity and severity, and often, by a joke or a laugh, breaks the force of offensive remarks, which cannot easily be overthrown by arguments.' Anyone who has ever made a speech will doubtless acknowledge that Cicero has a point: effective speakers tend to be those who can add levity at appropriate moments either to counterbalance excessive seriousness, or to establish a rapport with an audience; comedy is also useful for rendering audiences more receptive to potentially unpalatable remarks. However, Cicero makes it clear that an orator should be circumspect in the use of humour: 'to what

15 See Salvatore Attardo, *Linguistic Theories of Humor* (New York: Mouton De Gruyter, 1994) 24-26.

degree the laughable should be carried by the orator requires very diligent consideration [...] for neither great vice, such as is united with crime, nor great misery, is a subject for ridicule and laughter.'[16] A good orator is one who has a feel for what is appropriate; again, anyone who has tried to add levity to a public speech will know how easily tactlessness can destroy humour, and most people will have witnessed the negative effect of a joke being taken too far.

Cicero also made an interesting distinction between types of jokes: 'There are two sorts of jokes, one of which is excited by things, the other by words.' The jokes created by words (*in verbo*) are those born of puns, well–turned phrases, ambiguity, proverbs, figurative language, irony, and so on; jokes created by things or facts (*de re*) are those born of amusing situations. Cicero's reference to things and facts here does not mean that such comic situations need to adhere scrupulously to reality. On the contrary, he recognised that it is legitimate for speakers to stray from the literal facts when engaging in comedy. Indeed, according to Barry Sanders, it is Cicero who, 'establishes fiction [...] as the proper context for humour,' stressing the importance of achieving a 'vulgarized but accented imitation' in orations, and 'caricaturing in order to emphasise a point' (Barry Sanders, *Sudden Glory*, 120-1); in other words, it is perfectly acceptable to exaggerate, or even to make things up for comic effect. Cicero stresses the importance of using humour as a way of bringing situations to life, and any distortion of reality does not necessarily undermine it; in fact it is possible to arrive at a kind of truth via comic fabrication—it is possible, for instance, to reveal the essence of a character: 'the truth of a person [brought off by] fabricating every detail' (Cicero, *On the Orator*, quoted in Sanders, *Sudden Glory*, 122). Cicero felt that skilled rhetoricians are able to merge comic fabrication with believability, and argued that the former could be employed to enhance the latter. This is an interesting notion, and you can find this view of comedy—the notion that there's truth behind comic fabrication—throughout much of its history. As Chaucer wrote in 'The Cook's Tale,' 'A man may say full in game and play,' which

---

16 Cicero, *On the Orator*, trans. J.S. Watson (New York: Harper & Brother, 1875) 151.

is a variation of the old saying, 'many a true word is spoken in jest;' Shakespeare in *King Lear* makes the same point: 'Jesters do oft prove prophets.' In a similar vein, modern stand–up comedians and their fans often talk of stand–up as expressing a kind of truth. For instance, the American stand–up Lenny Bruce once said that, 'The only honest art form is laughter,' despite the fact that Bruce's own stand–up routines mostly took the form of bizarre fabrications. This is an important feature of comedy, or of people's perception of it, and we will return to it again later when discussing how humorous narrative itself can become a vehicle for philosophical thought.

Cicero is the first to fully appreciate the rhetorical power of humour; indeed he was the first to offer a substantial, systematic analysis of humour, and his writing influenced people's thinking about the subject, particularly in relation to rhetoric and oratory, well into the Renaissance. He is responsible for developing many of the terms and concepts used to discuss humour, including the term for jokes themselves, facetiae (plural of the Latin, *facetiae*), which means amusing narratives.

Creative Writing Exercise

Think of a recent experience in your life and write it out in the form of a literal narration: just simply describe it as a series of events, as they happened. It doesn't have to be anything dramatic. When it is complete, go back over the account and—without actually lying— see if there are any aspects of the narrative that you can alter in order to make it more entertaining. Exaggeration is a useful tool here. So, for instance, you might want to pick up on any signature traits of the people you encountered, and exaggerate them. This is called caricature. Think about your surroundings too and try to identify its most memorable, distinctive features: focus on striking specific details and, again, consider enhancing them via overstatement. Use comparisons, and images to amplify a sense of the presence of characters and their environment. It is sometimes worth imagining that you are telling the story to a friend whose attention you want to keep. The important thing is to find those aspects of the truth that can be tweaked in order to make them more vivid for your friend, whilst still reflecting your experience. If the experience has happened more than once, or is in any way similar to another experience you might have had, consider merging the most entertaining elements from each.

If you continue to embellish/exaggerate your experience, try to determine at what point it begins to feel overdone, or untrue. When you have reached this point try to determine in what sense it *is* untrue.

4. Superiority Theories of Humour

'Everything is funny as long as it is happening to someone else.' —Will Rogers.

The idea that laughter is linked to a sense of pleasure derived from other people's misfortune begins with Plato, as we have seen, and it is continued through Aristotle. Cicero also writes of how laughter can be employed to defeat an adversary, and advocates using comedy in a way that 'shatters obstructs or makes light of an opponent;' in other words to assert superiority. The foundations for a Superiority Theory of humour were laid in the ancient world, then, and these early views on laughter had a bearing on how later philosophers approached the subject.

4.1 Rene Descartes: The Benefits of Ridicule

The French philosopher and mathematician, Rene Descartes (1596–1650), is sometimes regarded as the first modern philosopher, and certainly he was the first to address the relationship between laughter and superiority substantially. He is not particularly interested in humour, as such, concentrating for the most part on laughter alone. His ideas on the subject can be found principally in his last published work, *The Passions of the Soul* (1649), where he offers an account of the physiology of laughter:

> Laughter consists in the fact that the blood, which proceeds from the right orifice in the heart by the arterial vein, inflating the lungs suddenly and repeatedly, causes the air which they contain to be constrained to pass out from them with an impetus by the windpipe, where it forms an inarticulate and explosive utterance [...] And it is just this action of the face with

this inarticulate and explosive voice that we call laughter.[17]

Descartes' conception of the bodily mechanics of laughter is out-dated, but his focus on its explosive nature is interesting, as is his notion that laughter accompanies a sudden expansion of the lungs, and an interruption of normal breathing. These are characteristics that for some denote the aggressive nature of laughter: it is 'explosive' and therefore potentially hostile. This is important because it distinguishes laughter from smiling: a significant distinction for humour theorists and one that is central to the ideas of some contemporary philosophers, as will be seen. Another feature of Descartes' view of laughter is that it involves the interaction of mind and body; laughter is caused by 'the surprise of admiration or wonder, which, being united by joy, may open the orifices of the heart so quickly [that it] inflates the lung' (René Descartes, *The Passions of the Soul*, Article 125). The corporeal dimension of laughter has troubled many over the years: the physicality of the experience, and the apparent loss of self–control associated with it, has been considered unseemly, if not positively dangerous at various points in history; also the physicality of laughter is one reason why religions have a record of being squeamish about it.

In *The Passions of the Soul* Descartes is also interested in the emotions: what form they take, what causes them, what significance they have, and how they relate to laughter. He associates laughter in particular with three emotions: wonder, joy, and hatred. Though he mentions wonder and joy as possible causes of laughter, he focuses mainly on laughter's association with the less positive emotion of hate, particularly in its relationship with scorn, derision, ridicule and mockery. These represent joy mixed with hatred for Descartes, who feels that joy alone is incapable of producing laughter. Thus while 'it seems as though laughter were one of the principle signs of joy,' joy can only create laughter when it 'has some wonder or hate mingled with it' (*The Passions*, Article 125).

For Descartes ridicule can have a positive social function when it takes the form of 'modest bantering,' as this exposes vices; as a

---

17 René Descartes, *The Passions of the Soul*, Part II, Article 124 (Quoted in John Morreall, ed., *The Philosophy of Laughter and Humor*, 21–22).

result he felt that it is perfectly permissible to laugh at other people, that the butt of a joke can actually deserve their derision, and that mocking laughter is socially responsible when it acts as a corrective to errant behaviour. Clearly there is an element of superiority in his view of the relationship between the joker and the butt's potential for improvement. While it is permissible for us to laugh at other people's jokes, however, we shouldn't laugh at our own because it is not fitting for us to appear surprised at the results of our own wit!

Creative Writing Exercise

Choose someone who you feel is morally lacking and, adopting their voice and character, write a letter to God attempting to justify the way they live their life. Errant politicians are often a good choice. Try to make them sound ridiculous by enlarging on what you feel are their transgressions. Remember Cicero's notion that it's possible to reveal the truth of a character via comedy. If you manage to write something that offers a successful humorous critique of that person, then you will have written a satire. The notion of superiority is central to satire of course: should you feel compelled to satirise someone it is generally because you feel superior to them and wish to improve society by exposing their shortcomings.

4.2 Thomas Hobbes: Sudden Glory

Pause and Reflect

Can you recall any humorous situations in which laughter wasn't in one way or another at someone else's expense? Do we always feel superior when we laugh?

Descartes' idea that humour can benefit society, and his willingness to associate it at least to a degree with emotions other than hatred, distinguishes him from the less compromising Superiority Theorist, Thomas Hobbes (1588–1679). While Hobbes didn't have that much to say about either humour or laughter, he is the key figure in the development of Superiority Theory, probably because he presented a succinct theory of laughter in an extremely lucid way. His theory needs to be seen in the context of his general theory of life and his belief that human beings are in a ceaseless struggle for power that only ends at death; for Hobbes humour assists individuals in their fight for power. He discusses laughter in *The Elements of Law Natural and Politic* (1650), where he refers to a 'passion which hath no name' and which is signalled by laughter:

> I may therefore conclude, that the passion of laughter is nothing else but a sudden glory arising from sudden conception of some eminency in ourselves, by comparison with the infirmities of others, or with our own formerly: for men laugh at the follies of themselves past, when they come suddenly to remembrance, except they bring with them any present dishonour.[18]

This is the clearest early statement of what has become known as Superiority Theory. For Hobbes, individuals laugh at their sense of other people's inferiority or absurdity; they laugh at a suddenly revealed shortcoming in others, in comparison with their own perceived sense of superiority. The emphasis on suddenness is presumably important in distinguishing feelings of superiority which produce laughter, from feelings of superiority which do not. It is only when eminence is abruptly/unexpectedly revealed that it has the desired effect. According to Hobbes people can also laugh at themselves, or rather their former selves, but only insofar as they recognise that they have moved on, and are now wiser and superior to that former self. He also felt that when people laugh at their own jokes, they are laughing at their skill in making that joke, and the sense of superiority they derive from that ('a sudden conception of some ability in himself.')

Hobbes believed that laughter is a product of malicious enjoyment at our own sense of triumph, then, and that there is always a degree of conflict and antagonism associated with it. As a consequence he objected to laughter on moral grounds, and didn't think much of those who laugh at other people's expense, feeling that such laughter tends to be a sign of cowardliness. There *are* forms of humour that are relatively benign, in that they don't cause offence, but it seems

---

18 Thomas Hobbes, *The Elements of Law Natural and Politic* (1650), chapter IX (available at thomas-hobbes.com), unpaginated.

that superiority is at work here too:

> Laughter without offence must be at absurdities and infirmities abstracted from persons, and where all the company may laugh together. For laughing to one's self putteth all the rest to a jealousy and examination of themselves; besides, it is vain glory, and an argument of little worth, to think the infirmities of another sufficient matter for his triumph. (Thomas Hobbes, *The Elements,* Chapter IX, 1650)

Laughter evoked by absurdity and infirmity is less negative when it isn't directed at specific people, and when it is common to all present. However, it is difficult not to feel that Hobbes is close to undermining his own theory here, particularly with his reference to absurdities 'abstracted from persons.' It is not a huge step to assume the possibility of people laughing at the concept of absurdity itself, rather than at absurd people as such. In social situations the object of laughter is surely not always someone we're comparing ourselves to, and we do indeed often appear to be laughing at something that is, to use Hobbes's term, 'abstracted from persons.' John Lippitt makes this point: 'When a loving parent laughs at the linguistic blunders committed by small children ('chish and fips'; 'par carks'), one can accept that there is a definite sense in which the parent is superior to the child, without accepting that this is *why* he or she is amused.'[19] In such situations it seems plausible to assume that we are laughing at absurdity for its own sake, and when this is the case surely the concept of superiority is irrelevant? In one sense, then, the answer to the question posed at the beginning of this section, 'Do we always feel superior when we laugh?' would appear to be no.

Creative Writing Exercise

Write a comic short story about a good-looking, intelligent character living in a picturesque town. Now write another comic short story featuring an ugly character who is not very bright living in the same picturesque town. Which story is easiest to write, and which is the most successful? Is ugly funnier than beautiful?

---

19 John Lippitt, 'Humour and Superiority.' See online resources.

4.3 Henri Bergson: The Mechanical Encrusted on the Living

Pause and Reflect

We often laugh at things that are out–of–step with the norm (for instance someone who talks or walks in an odd way), or when the norm is in some way overstated (for instance through excessive repetition). Think about why this might be so. The French philosopher Henry Bergson (1859–1941) thought he had an answer.

Henri Bergson is an immensely significant figure in the history of humour theory, and one of the few pre–twenty first century philosophers to devote a book–length study to the subject: *Laughter: An Essay on the Meaning of the Comic* (1900). Despite the reference to laughter in the title, his emphasis is less on laughter and more on humour and how it is created. As with Hobbes, Bergson's views need to be understood in relation to his general philosophy, particularly his opinion that human beings are animated by something called *Élan vital*: a vital force driving both evolution and creativity. According to Bergson we have an intuitive awareness of this force, and an understanding of its essential nature, but whenever we lose sight of it we also lose sight of our humanness. In short, the comic is associated with those moments when we *do* lose sight of it, and laughter becomes our prompt to rediscover it again.

For Bergson laughter is exclusively human: we only laugh at things that are either human or that are given significance by their relationship to humans. So if we laugh at an animal it is only because it has become humanised in some way. He argues that humour requires a degree of indifference too, and that emotions like sentimentality, affection, and pity tend to inhibit it. Laughter is also a communal phenomenon for Bergson: it thrives among people, and not in one person in isolation. We are a source of laughter when we are out of step with the social norm, and as soon as we become aware of that fact we adjust our behaviour accordingly:

> when people perceive ridiculousness in themselves they take action to modify their behaviour; jesting at their expense can

bring it to their attention, of course, and hence laughter can 'correct man's manners.' [20]

For Bergson, to function socially we require an awareness of our situation in the world, and an ability to adapt to our world where necessary. There are two forces at work in healthy individuals: 'tension' and 'elasticity;' the latter enables flexibility and adaptation, and whenever humans reveal themselves as *inelastic* they are a potential source of comedy. Human beings are not content merely to live, they strive to live in the best way possible; this necessitates flexibility, and because society is conscious of this requirement, it abhors complacency and the 'easy automatism of acquired habits.' Society looks down on those lacking the elasticity to adapt to necessary social developments: 'it insists on a constant striving after reciprocal adaptation.' So for Bergson laughter is created when we perceive instances of people's inability to adapt to their social circumstances; laughing at people is socially acceptable way of identifying and criticising inflexibility. Bergson feels that laughter keeps alive something essential in human beings, it 'keeps constantly awake and in mutual contact certain activities of a secondary order which [if not for laughter] might retire into their shell and go to sleep,' and in this way, 'laughter pursues a utilitarian role of general improvement' (Henri Bergson, *Laughter*, 23–24). So this is clearly a Superiority Theory of humour in the sense that people who behave correctly laugh at those who behave incorrectly, and Bergson's view is a little like Descartes' in that he feels laughter can be edifying and improving.

Bergson's theory might sound a bit strange, and it probably needs a little more explanation; with his notion of rigidity versus elasticity in mind, consider the following words:

> To sum up, whatever be the doctrine to which our reason assents, our imagination has a very clear–cut philosophy of its own: in every human form it sees the effort of a soul which is shaping matter, a soul which is infinitely supple and perpetually in motion, subject to no law of gravitation, for it is

---

20 Henri Bergson, *Laughter: An Essay on the Meaning of the Comic* Trans. Cloudesley Brereton and Fred Rothwell (London: Green Integer Books, 1900) 21.

not the earth that attracts it. This soul imparts a portion of its winged lightness to the body it animates: the immateriality which thus passes into matter is what is called gracefulness. Matter, however, is obstinate and resists. It draws to itself the ever–alert activity of this higher principle, would fain convert it to its own inertia and cause it to revert to mere automatism. It would fain immobilize the intelligently varied movements of the body in stupidly contracted grooves, stereotype in permanent grimaces the fleeting expressions of the face, in short imprint on the whole person such an attitude as to make it appear immersed and absorbed in the materiality of some mechanical occupation instead of ceaselessly renewing its vitality by keeping in touch with a living ideal. Where matter thus succeeds in dulling the outward life of the soul, in petrifying its movements and thwarting its gracefulness, it achieves, at the expense of the body, an effect that is comic. If, then, at this point we wished to define the comic by comparing it with its contrary, we should have to contrast it with gracefulness even more than with beauty. It partakes rather of the unsprightly than of the unsightly, of *rigidness* rather than of *ugliness*. (Henri Bergson, *Laughter*, 30–1)

Laughter is created when the soul is in conflict with the body. There is something transcendent and infinitely flexible that informs humankind, but this sometimes clashes with our awkward material selves: the latter can inhibit this flexibility and render it mechanical and repetitive. Laughter is what keeps us 'in touch with a living ideal' by alerting us to the threat of stasis and the negative mindset of rigidity and repetition. Rigidity is funny, but it is also unwelcome, and laughter reminds us of this. So the ugliest faces are not necessarily the funniest for Bergson: the funniest are those which suggest rigidity, such as a fixed expression that implies a preoccupation with a single thought. He explains the humorous appeal of caricature in this way: a normal face is never fixed or perfect because it is animated by *Élan vital*, but caricaturists make them fixed by picking up on a telling trait, and reducing the whole face to that single characteristic. When this happens, stasis is at odds with *Élan vital*, and the consequence is laughter. This notion could be used to explain the comic possibilities of any type of imitation, as imitation is only really possible insofar as something exhibits predictability and rigidity. Once again, repeatable behaviour conflicts with the vital human spirit because, as Bergson suggests, 'the really living life shall never repeat itself' (Henri Bergson, *Laughter*, 35). Similarly any form of ritual or ceremony always has the potential for humour because they too are dependent on repetition; indeed this applies to any form of adherence to routine. To illustrate the latter, Bergson cites the case of a shipwreck from which a number of passengers were saved by customs–house officials; upon saving them the officers asked the passengers if they had anything to declare. This is funny because the customs officers so rigidly stick to the rules of their occupation, behaving like automata rather than human beings. Clothes can also undermine our *Élan vital* because they conflict with the 'winged lightness' that the soul imparts on the body, undermining its gracefulness. We tend not to notice this when clothes are in fashion, because then there is a degree of compatibility between the wearer and the garment. However, when a garment is out of fashion it draws attention to itself, foregrounding the fact that nature has been tampered with: on such occasions, says Bergson, we will have witnessed, 'the soul tantalized by the needs of the body: on the one hand the moral personality with its intelligently varied energy, and, on the other, the stupidly monotonous body, perpetually obstructing everything with its machine like obstinacy.' (Henri Bergson, *Laughter*, 50).

The starting point for the comic for Bergson, then, is 'when something mechanical' is 'encrusted on the living,' both in relation to living individuals, and the living community as a whole (Henri Bergson, *Laughter*, 49). The comic is associated with 'automatism,' and the characteristics of comedy demonstrate this mechanical quality. He lists three characteristics in particular, arguing that something 'may become comic either by *repetition*, by *inversion*, or by *reciprocal interference*' (Henri Bergson, Laughter, 109). The first two speak for themselves, but by 'reciprocal interference' he means 'bracketing in the same expression two independent meanings that apparently tally,' an example of which would be a play on words such as a pun. These three all imply inflexibility: repetition suggests duplication without variation, inversion suggests the expectation of duplication, and a play on words breaks down the sense of harmony that we feel 'exists between language and nature,' undermining the natural fluency of language (Henri Bergson, *Laughter,* 111). The so-called 'rule of three' in humour is one example of repetition; jokes are often structured around threes, with the repetition signalling comic intent (an Englishman, Irishman, and a Scotsman, etc.). Stand–up comedians also often use repetition to structure their monologues: there is a technique sometimes called 'reincorporation' or 'call back' which involves comedians apparently moving away from a particular topic, only to come back to it again at various points throughout the performance. Sometimes they may pretend to be comically obsessed with the reincorporated topic. Inversions are common in humour too, of course; Bergson is interested in inversions that depend on a pattern having being established in recipient's mind, implying the expectation of repetition which is undermined when the expected item is turned on its head. Word play which establishes a duel meaning is also a standard comic device (for instance, 'a good pun is its own reword'); as suggested Bergson sees this as violating the relationship between language and the world. The following joke might be said to employ all three of Bergson's comic elements:

> Three nuns were walking down the road. Out from the bushes jumped a flasher. They were shocked! The first one had a stroke. The second one had a stroke. The third one couldn't reach it.

This joke is underpinned by repetition, stressed by the count of three. It inverts our expectations too, turning the idea that the nuns are morally shocked on its head. This inversion only works because it undermines repeated behaviour (the normal behaviour of nuns). It also includes 'reciprocal interference' in the form of word play, employing a single word with different meanings within the same expression: the word 'stroke' here means both brain haemorrhage and sexual stimulation simultaneously.

As suggested, Bergson's ideas are compatible with Superiority

Theory in that the laughter created by the comic works to mock those who demonstrate inflexibility, and humiliate them into readjustment; in this sense humour and laughter have a positive social role. As will be seen, however, his ideas also have much in common with Incongruity Theory, so much so that he could legitimately be considered as part of that tradition too.

Creative Writing Exercise

With the comic possibilities of inflexibility in mind, create a character whose life is governed by an amusing obsession. Their life can be normal in every other respect, but their obsession dominates their activities. Write a day in the life of your character. Begin by listing their actions throughout the day, and use the list as a foundation for the story. You should find that there are lots of comic possibilities, and many different ways in which you could develop the story. As a way of ending the story you might consider exploiting the reader's expectations and inverting some aspect of the repeated activity.

4.4 Humour as a Game

Pause and Reflect

Is there always an element of competition in humorous situations? Can you think of any occasions for humour that don't seem to have a competitive aspect?

Superiority Theories of the kind discussed above have influenced more recent theorists, including some who, like Albert Rapp, strive to formulate evolutionary models of laughter. In *The Origins of Wit and Humor* (1951) Rapp argues that laughter is a civilised expression of the triumphant cry which, for our primitive ancestors, signalled victory over an opponent. He coined the term 'thrashing laughter' to describe this, and maintains that in the modern world physical conflicts have been relocated to the arena of social humour, and 'thrashing laughter' can still be heard when a social adversary is bested in a battle of wits. The American academic, Charles Gruner takes Rapp's evolutionary laughter theory as a starting point. In books like

Understanding Laughter (1978) and *The Game of Humor* (1997), he argues that laughter and humour are invariably about winning, and like Rapp he suggests that joking and laughter take the place of physical combat in the modern world. His aim has partly been to defend humour from the negative implications of Superiority Theory, and the belief that humour and laughter are socially unacceptable just because they involve conflict and assertions of status. As the title of his second book suggests, he draws parallels between humour and games, claiming that humour is enjoyable for the same reasons they are: 'The very idea of a game implies fun, leisure, entertainment, recreation, affable human interaction;' but this doesn't mean they too don't have a primitive element, as gaming 'also implies competition, keeping score and a winner and a loser.'[21] Gaming isn't considered anti–social, and equally there is no reason why we should be squeamish about laughter, regardless of its association with superiority. It is certainly true that a sense of competition seems to be useful to humour writers. When comedy writers work in teams, for instance, there is often a competitive element which spurs each writer to try and go one better than their collaborators. All humour writers are familiar with the concept of 'topping the joke'; that is, taking a comic idea as far as it can go and extracting every last grain of comic potential from it. Perhaps this phenomenon goes some way toward supporting Gruner's thesis.

Creative Writing Exercise

> Joke-topping is a useful technique that can be employed by writers even when they're working alone. You can develop comic ideas simply by asking, 'what would be even funnier than this?' Always be prepared to go back to your work and try to outdo your last effort. With this is mind, imagine a scene where two comedy writers are collaborating on a story in which a character is being searched by a doorman before entry into a nightclub. The two writers are arguing about the funniest thing that could be discovered in their character's pocket. Have your two comedy writers try to outdo one another. As you develop the dialogue you will find yourself 'topping the joke.'

21 Charles Gruner, *The Game of Humor: A Comprehensive Theory of Why We Laugh'* (New Jersey: Transaction Publishers, 1997) 2.

Charles Gruner extends Superiority Theory to all examples of humour, claiming that it applies in all situations. He went so far as to pose an annual challenge to The International Society for Humor Studies, inviting them to produce an example of humour that he 'could not render "dehumorized" by removing its contest nature'—a challenge that he extends to readers of his book (Gruner, *The Game of Humor*, 176). Those who contest Superiority Theory sometimes cite examples of verbal ingenuity like puns as evidence that superiority doesn't always apply to humour, but even here Gruner sees hierarchy and conflict: 'creators of puns and punning riddles do so in order to "defeat" their targets/publics with brilliant verbal expressionism' (Gruner, *The Game of Humor*, 145). He also argues against those like Christopher Wilson who, in *Jokes, Form, Content, Use and Function* (1979), claims that nonsense is a form of humour devoid of superiority or aggression because it creates amusement solely via incongruity. Gruner disagrees and deems instances of nonsense such as Spoonerisms (for example, 'you hissed my mystery lecture' as opposed to 'you missed my history lecture') to be mere speech errors that are amusing *because* they are errors, implying stupidity. He makes a similar case against so–called childish humour ('what does blue look like from behind?'), and jokes that are oxymoronic ('I'd give my right arm to be ambidextrous'), all of which don't seem to have any element of superiority. For Gruner, 'these jokes are funny only because of the stupidity of their authors,' and if we laugh we are laughing because of our sense of the joker's inferiority (Gruner, *The Game of Humor*, 155–6). This brings us back to the point made above about the necessity of having to compare ourselves to others in order for such things to be amusing; does the 'author' or the imagined speaker of such jokes have any bearing on their capacity to generate laughter, or is it possible to laugh merely at absurdity itself? Gruner's theory suggests that absurdity in and of itself is not funny: it demands a human context and a hierarchy, be it real or imagined.

Creative Writing Exercise

All of the Superiority Theorists discussed so far would agree that a character's potential to create humour partly depends on them appearing inferior to us in some way. Take a character based on someone you know and try putting them into a context in which they could not help but look ridiculous. A crude example might be someone who cannot sing placed in a situation where they are forced to perform a song. It is a good idea to experiment with point-of-view: try writing it in the third and the first person, and from different characters' perspectives. If you manage to create a scene that you feel is amusing, think about the nature of the humour: does it rely on your reader feeling superior? Would there be a way of rewriting the scene so that we felt admiration for the character, without losing the humour? Read the next section with this problem in mind.

4.5 Roger Scruton: Attentive Demolition

A contemporary philosopher whose work draws on Superiority Theory, but who ultimately dismisses it is Roger Scruton. In his essay, 'Laughter,' he agrees that laughter devalues its object in the eyes of the one who laughs, which is why while most people enjoy laughing, few relish being laughed at. However, there are many ways in which we can be said to laugh at things. It is true that scorn and mockery can elicit laughter, of course, but for Scruton such laughter has a 'quality of malice which can be heard or overheard only with revulsion.'[22] Sarcasm too suggests a degree of malevolence that renders it difficult to enjoy; but he makes a noteworthy distinction between sarcasm and irony. Scruton points out that while irony is similar to sarcasm in some respects, in one important sense it is different. While it might be true that irony devalues the object, it does not also reject the object in the way that sarcasm does; in short, sarcasm is invariably negative, but irony is not. Using James Joyce's *Ulysses* (1922) as an example, he points to the ironic comparison Joyce makes between his protagonist, Leopold Bloom, and Homer's Odysseus. It is ironic, of course, because Bloom is not a hero in the way that Homer's character is. However, readers tend to feel more affection for Leopold Bloom as a result of that contrast, *even though* the irony diminishes him by comparison. The irony creates a degree of pathos in relation to Bloom

---

22 Roger Scruton, 'Laughter,' in John Morreall, ed., *The Philosophy of Laughter and Humor* (New York: State University of New York Press) 168.

and, according to Scruton:

> His shortcomings are part of this pathos, since they reflect a
> condition that is also ours. Irony of this kind causes us to laugh
> at its object only by laughing at ourselves. It forces upon us
> a perception of our own kinship. (Roger Scruton, 'Laughter,'
> 168)

We feel more positive toward Bloom as a result of him being affec-
tionately mocked by Joyce, and we do so because we are reminded of
our own frailties and our own lowly status as human beings.

Amusement for Scruton is a 'pattern of thought' that he calls
'attentive demolition.' This phrase brings to mind Superiority Theory
of course, but he takes pains to deny this association: he argues that
'attentive demolition' does not create a Hobbesian hierarchy but, as
seen with the example of irony in Joyce, a sense of 'kinship' between
subject and object. The problem with Superiority Theories for Scruton
is that they:

> find the meaning of humour in what it does for the subject,
> rather than in how it represents the object. Humour is not,
> normally, self–directed. Indeed one of its values lies in the
> fact that it directs our attention unceasingly outwards. If we
> are repelled by the humourless person it is often because we
> think of him as interested only in himself. (Roger Scruton,
> 'Laughter,' 169)

Humour is not as self–interested as Superiority Theorists suggest; in
fact it most often steers us away from ourselves. Also it often has the
effect of humanising, rather that denigrating its object. Fun at an individual's expense may actually be a necessary thing, and something
that might be welcomed by that individual; after all, who wants to be
perceived as 'interested only in himself'? For instance, Scruton won-
ders if it would even be possible to love someone who was genuinely
flawless, a so–called 'great man,' in a normal way. In order to love
them 'it may be necessary to find in him that which can be (however
gently) laughed at;' and then if that individual were 'truly great', they
would 'be willing to exchange the absolute security of the unlaugh-
able for the comfort of human affection.' (Roger Scruton, 'Laughter,'

168). So while the notion of 'demolition' suggests superiority, hier-archy, and aggression, it can actually be about rendering individuals more human, and therefore more likeable. So in answer to the ques-tion posed in the last writing exercise, it should actually be possible to write a comic scene in which the so–called butt of a joke is human-ised rather than undermined by ridicule. To take the example of a tone-deaf singer who performs before an audience: we may laugh at his inability to sing and his foolishness for making himself a figure of fun, but if his behaviour were to remind us of our own capacity to compromise our dignity then we may be inclined to qualify our sense of superiority; we might even feel this is an attractive facet of his personality which enables us to identify with him on a human level. In short we would like him more because he is more like us, and the humour will work to augment rather than diminish him in our eyes.

Creative Writing Exercise

> Now that you know something about Roger Scruton's take on Superiority Theory, have another go at rewriting the scene from the last exercise. This time try to use your ridiculous character's comic predicament to reveal a frailty that might make your reader inclined to identify with him/her. You can do this via irony perhaps, making sure that your reader sees more about your character than your character sees.

5. Incongruity Theory

5.1 Frances Hutcheson and James Beattie

As suggested, Aristotle and Cicero both make statements that are compatible with Incongruity Theory, but it was Frances Hutcheson (1694–1746) who developed it more fully in the eighteenth century. In *Reflections Upon Laughter* (1750) he took issue with Hobbes's Superiority Theory on a number of points. He challenged Hobbes's notion that laughter always requires a comparison of ourselves to others on the grounds that we sometimes laugh when other human beings don't appear to be involved at all. For instance, when we laugh at the written words of an author (Hutcheson cites Homer), we might be inclined to ask: to whom are we comparing ourselves, and to whom do we feel superior? Also, if it were true that all sudden experiences of superiority create laughter, then wouldn't we be laughing more often? Not only that, but if Hobbes is correct then surely the more superior we feel towards someone or something, the greater the potential for humour; but this is not our experience. Hutcheson illustrates this by reminding us that in the animal kingdom the funniest animals are not necessarily the ones to which we feel more superior; animals that remind us of ourselves are the funniest: so, for instance, a dog is funnier than an oyster; a monkey is funnier than an amoeba. After dismissing Hobbes he begins to develop his own philosophy of humour, and signs of an incipient Incongruity Theory can be seen here:

> That then which seems generally the cause of laughter is the bringing together of images which have contrary additional ideas, as well as some resemblance in the principal idea: this contrast between ideas of grandeur, dignity, sanctity, perfection and ideas of meanness, baseness, profanity, seems to be

the very spirit of burlesque; and the greatest part of our rail-
lery and jest are founded upon it.[23]

Notice how he explains humour with reference to a coming together
of things that are incompatible, particularly the contrast between high
and low ('sanctity' and 'profanity,' etc.). Hutcheson expands on this
by discussing the type of humour created when serious people lose
their dignity:

> any little accident to which we have joined the idea of mean-
> ness, befalling a person of great gravity, ability, dignity, is a
> matter of laughter [...] thus the strange contortions of the body
> in the fall, the dirtying of a decent dress, the natural functions
> which we study to conceal from sight, are matters of laughter
> when they occur to observation in persons of whom we have
> high ideas. (Frances Hutcheson 'From *Reflections*,' 33)

The focus is on the contrast between notions of reserve, solemnity,
and dignity, on the one hand, and with awkwardness on the other: it
is a juxtaposition of conflicting images—an incongruity—that creates the laughter.

Creative Writing Exercise

Create a character for whom dignity is important and come up with
some situations in which this could be undermined to comic effect.
Once you have dignity or gravity as defining character traits you will
find it is easy to generate humour by placing the character in contexts
where these are compromised. Situations of this kind can be used
to create bathos: a shift from the exalted to the commonplace.
Hutcheson would argue that it is not the hierarchy that creates the
humour but our perception of the contrast between high and low.

Pause and Reflect

It is certainly true that many jokes and humorous situations involve
contrasts and incongruities of various kinds. Think about some of the

---

23 Frances Hutcheson 'From *Reflections Upon Laughter*,' in John Morreall, ed.,
The Philosophy of Laughter and Humor (New York: State University of New York
Press, 1987) 32.

jokes and humour you are familiar with and try to identify incongru- ity. Look for something that is incompatible with something else. What clashes with what? Are all incongruities funny?

One of the first philosophers to actually use the term 'incongru- ity' when discussing laughter is the Scottish philosopher, James Beattie (1735–1803). In an essay called 'On Laughter and Ludicrous Composition' (1776), he writes:

> Laughter arises from the view of two or more inconsistent, unsuitable, or incongruous parts or circumstances, considered as united in one complex object or assemblage, or as acquiring a sort of mutual relation from the peculiar manner in which the mind takes notice of them.[24]

This implies that laughter is created by two incompatible concepts which—within the frame of a joke or humorous situation—are momentarily perceived as being in some way compatible (having 'mutual relation'). Interestingly it suggests that incongruity alone is not enough to create laughter; the incongruous elements must be seen to fit together on one level, as a result of 'the peculiar manner in which the mind takes notice of them.' You only have to think about incongruity for a little while to realise that not all incongruities are funny.

5.2 Immanuel Kant: Transformations into Nothing

The German philosopher Immanuel Kant (1724–1804) developed an Incongruity Theory of humour in his *Critique of Judgement* (1790). His discussion of humour focuses on jokes, emphasising the physical pleasure we enjoy when we perceive an incongruity. Typically a joke sets up an expectation in the form of a narrative build–up, and then undermines this with a punch line. In Kant's words, 'laughter is an affection arising from the sudden transformation of a strained expec- tation into nothing.' For Kant the joke process constitutes a form of 'play with aesthetic ideas' which animate the body via the mind; it

24 Quoted in Rod A. Martin, *The Psychology of Humor: An Integrative Approach* (London: Elsevier Academic Press, 2007) 63.

creates laughter and a 'feeling of health produced by a motion of the intestines.' When we hear a joke, he says:

> The play begins with the thoughts which together occupy the body, so far as they admit of sensible expression; and as the understanding stops suddenly short at this presentment, in which it does not find what it expected, we feel the effect of this slackening in the body by oscillations of the organs, which promotes the restoration of equilibrium and has a favourable influence on health. [25]

Consider the following joke, which in a 2001 survey conducted by Professor Richard Wiseman of the University of Hertfordshire, was voted the world's funniest:

> A couple of New Jersey hunters are out in the woods when one of them falls to the ground. He doesn't seem to be breathing; his eyes are rolled back in his head. The other guy whips out his cell phone and calls the emergency services. He gasps to the operator: 'My friend is dead! What can I do?' The operator, in a calm soothing voice says: 'Just take it easy. I can help. First, let's make sure he's dead.'
>
> There is a silence, and then a shot is heard. The guy's voice comes back on the line. He says: 'OK, now what?' [26]

We can see how the expectation is established in the first paragraph, specifically in its final line, 'let's make sure he's dead;' our expectation—namely that the hunter is going to check his friend's pulse—is abruptly undermined in the punch line. The joke suddenly resolves the tension established in the narrative by negating it; in other words, it turns the 'strained expectation into nothing,' by transforming it into a joke. As suggested, there is a sense of physical release or relief associated with humour for Kant, and here he has something in common with thinkers who feel that humour is associated with letting off steam, and who will be discussed more fully later.

---

25 Immanuel Kant, *Critique of Judgement*, trans., James Creed Meredith (New York: Cosimo Inc, 2007) 133.

26 For details of Richard Wiseman's research see the bibliography under online material.

Creative Writing Exercise

Try to write a comic scene which has a build-up/transformation structure like the New Jersey Hunter joke: set up an expectation and then undermine it. Try experimenting with the length of the narrative build-up compared to the punch line. You'll probably find that while you have some latitude to increase the extent of the build-up, there will be a limit to this before the tension begins to wane: you can only strain expectation so far, and there is a balance to be struck between holding a listener/reader in suspense, and boring them. You will also probably find that the punch line needs to be succinct and abrupt rather than protracted. As with Superiority Theory, suddenness is important. Obviously this is what humourists are referring to when they talk about timing.

Comic incongruities are often at odds with logic and rationality, of course: clearly in the case of the New Jersey hunter, his action defies reason. However, for Kant there was no pleasure to be found in this aspect of joking. The enjoyment of humour is derived solely from the physical pleasure that it creates in the individual, and not from the disruption reason. Kant was an Enlightenment figure, strongly devoted to reason, and as such did not feel that it was possible to equate intellectual gratification with irrationality. In this sense his differs from another important Incongruity Theorist, Arthur Schopenhauer (1788–1860).

5.3 Arthur Schopenhauer: Pleasure in the Defeat of Reason

Arthur Schopenhauer mentions humour in his most important book, *The World as Will and Idea* (1818). For Schopenhauer humour is born of a clash between what he calls the 'sensuous', on the one hand, and 'abstract knowledge' on the other. Basically he thinks that the version of the world that we are able to hold in our heads never truly matches what our senses tell us; the former 'merely approximate' to the latter, 'as a mosaic approximates to painting'. The incongruity between the two is the cause of laughter:

> The cause of laughter in every case is simply the sudden perception of the incongruity between a concept and the real

objects which have been thought through it in some relation, and laughter itself is just the expression of this incongruity.[27]

Where Kant felt that jokes disappear into nothing, they become a corrective to perception for Schopenhauer: humour is created when our view of the world is qualified; when we are forced to readjust our assumptions about it. For Schopenhauer, the punch line doesn't negate, it contributes to the import of the joke and the shift in understanding that gives it its force. So when it comes to the New Jersey hunter joke cited above, the concept might relate to the ideas we have about people and our ideal view of how they should behave—in other words not like idiots—but this concept is qualified in the punch line where we are presented with the reality that idiocy exists. Notice too that Schopenhauer talks about 'perception' and 'thought' in his discussion of incongruity; these are words which allow for a degree subjectivity in our responses to humour: after all, our experience tells us that the success of humour often depends a great deal on cultural factors and a shared understanding of the world.

An important distinction between Schopenhauer and Kant has to do with the latter's attitude to reason. As suggested, Kant feels that humour can only be enjoyed for its physical effects, and not for its own sake; in other words not simply for the cognitive thrill of having logic and reason usurped by incongruity; Kant felt that human reason is always going to conflict with the absurdity of humour. By contrast Schopenhauer was not a child of the Enlightenment and was less enamoured with reason. He has more in common with thinkers associated with Romanticism, for whom a strict adherence to reason felt limiting. Unlike Kant, Schopenhauer has no problem with incongruity offering an affront to reason: for him humour is created when concepts held in the mind are qualified by concrete reality; in other words, when humour reveals the inadequacy of reason, and we experience a pleasurable release from its misleading complexities. Unlike Kant he feels that there is pleasure to be gained from the defeat of reason.

Schopenhauer also makes an interesting distinction between folly

---

27 Arthur Schopenhauer, *The World as Will and Idea,*' Book I, 13, trans. R.B. Haldane and John Kemp (London: Routledge and Kegan Paul, 1907) 76.

and wit that is worth mentioning. With folly he suggests that: 'The concept is first present in knowledge, and we pass from it to reality, and to operation upon it, to action' (Arthur Schopenhauer, *The World as Will and Idea*, 77). In other words we have assumptions about the world, and when we act on these only to have them undermined by reality, we are guilty of folly. The example of the New Jersey hunter might constitute an example of folly in this sense: the hunter has a limited understanding (concept) of what the phrase, 'make sure he is dead' might mean, but he acts on this, passing from the concept to reality, and thus his folly creates humour. Schopenhauer contrasts this with what he calls wit. Wit is occasioned when 'we have previously known two or more very different real objects, ideas or sense perceptions and have identified them through the unity of a concept which comprehends them both.' For an example consider the following joke:

A woman gets on a bus with her baby.

The bus driver says: 'That's the ugliest baby that I've ever seen. Ugh!'

The woman goes to the rear of the bus and sits down, fuming. She says to a man next to her: 'The driver just insulted me!

The man says: 'You go right up there and tell him off: go ahead, I'll hold your monkey for you.'[28]

In Schopenhauer's terms we might say that two real objects—a baby and a monkey—are being deliberately identified through the unity of one concept—a monkey baby—which 'comprehends them both'. Of course we are working on the assumption that the man is aware that the baby is not a real monkey! Note that in the case of both folly and wit, incongruity is central to the humour: in the first instance it is a mismatch between assumption and reality, in the second it takes the form of two incongruous objects united in a single concept.

Creative Writing Exercise

Create an example of folly and an example of wit that you think

---

28 This joke was voted the funniest UK joke in Richard Wiseman's study.

would satisfy Schopenhauer's criteria.

5.4 Søren Kierkegaard

The Danish philosopher Søren Kierkegaard (1813–1855) also developed a version of Incongruity Theory. It was his belief that comedy is fundamental to life because, like life, it is born of contradictions. Kierkegaard thought that tragedy is also about contradictions, but comedy and tragedy differ because while 'tragedy is the suffering contradiction,' comedy is a 'painless contradiction.'[29] While tragedy cannot see a way of resolving contradictions, comedy can. There is always a degree of inevitability about a tragic hero's fate: they are on a trajectory that will end in death and there is no escaping this. Comedy, by contrast, is born of a *resolvable* contradiction: 'the comic apprehension evokes the contradiction or makes it manifest by having in mind the way out, which is why the contradiction is painless.' (Kierkegaard, 'Concluding Unscientific Postscript,' 83–4). So while, say, satire involves a contradiction between errant behaviour, on the one hand, and correct or ideal behaviour on the other, it also implies a 'way out' of this contradiction: namely that the object of the satire adjusts their behaviour. With this in mind, consider the following joke:

> Sherlock Holmes and Dr. Watson go on a camping trip. After a good dinner and a bottle of wine, they retire for the night, and go to sleep. Some hours later, Holmes wakes up and nudges his faithful friend. 'Watson, look up at the sky and tell me what you see.'
>
> 'I see millions and millions of stars, Holmes' replies Watson.
>
> 'And what do you deduce from that?'
>
> Watson ponders for a minute. 'Well, astronomically, it tells me that there are millions of galaxies and potentially billions of planets. Astrologically, I observe that Saturn is in Leo.

---

29 Søren Kierkegaard, 'Concluding Unscientific Postscript,' in John Morreall ed., *The Philosophy of Laughter and Humor* (New York: State University of New York Press, 1987) 83–89 (83).

Horologically, I deduce that the time is approximately a quarter past three. Meteorologically, I suspect that we will have a beautiful day tomorrow. Theologically, I can see that God is all powerful, and that we are a small and insignificant part of the universe. What does it tell you, Holmes?'

Holmes is silent for a moment. 'Watson, you idiot!' he says, 'Someone has stolen our tent!'[30]

At the heart of the humour here is a contradiction between our assumption that Watson is making pertinent observations of a kind that will appeal to Holmes, and the fact that Holmes is more interested in their missing tent. It is a painless contradiction in that it is resolvable if Watson makes a simple adjustment to his priorities.

Importantly, however, contradiction is not the only thing responsible for humour in this Holmes and Watson joke; amusement is created also as a result of the language Watson uses: it is the language we associate with Holmes, and it is fitting that Watson should use such language as he mimics his friend's method of logical deduction. In fact part of the humour depends on the fact that the language is indeed fitting in this sense; in other words, the humour is also partly dependent on an element of *congruity*. This brings us to one of several important problems with Incongruity Theory.

5.5 Problems with Incongruity Theory

Roger Scruton, whose essay 'Laughter' has been discussed above, takes issue with Incongruity Theory precisely because humour often depends on a certain fit between the joke and reality: in other words the humour actually depends on a kind of congruity. Scruton illustrates his objection with reference to caricature, pointing out that the latter is amusing not because there is a mismatch between a caricature and its object, but because there is a fit: 'If one wishes to describe the humour of a caricature in terms of incongruity it must be added that it is an incongruity which illustrates a deeper congruity between an object and itself' (Roger Scruton, 'Laughter,' 161). So this is one problem with Incongruity Theory, but there are others.

30 In Richard Wiseman's study, this joke was voted the second funniest of all time.

Incongruity Theories of humour tend to privilege the structure of humour over the content, suggesting that the structural dissonance itself is funny. It is true that there are recurring joke structures: knock knock jokes, Doctor Doctor jokes, and so on, where the positioning of the concepts seems to be a factor in their status as humorous. However, the fact that some of these jokes are funnier than others, clearly implies that something other than structural incongruity is at work. Another problem with Incongruity Theory has to do with the obvious fact that, as suggested above, not all incongruities are funny. Some are sad, some are sickening, and some are terrifying. If my legs suddenly turned to liquorish and I fell down the stairs and put my head through the television, I doubt if I would find it particularly amusing, despite my ability to identify a variety of surprising incongruities in the event.

Another problem with Incongruity Theory has to do with the fact that incongruities disrupt logic and reason. Some philosophers argue that it is not possible for human beings to take pleasure in such disruptions: we are psychologically incapable of enjoying the irrationality that accompanies discrepancies of logic and reason. As suggested earlier, Kant felt that humorous pleasure can only ever be physical, and many philosophers have picked up on this notion and taken it further. The Spanish–American philosopher George Satayana (1863–1952) was one of the first to discuss this objection to Incongruity Theory in depth, arguing that 'man, being a rational animal, can like absurdity no better than he can like hunger or cold;' and incongruity as such is always undesirable:

> Things amuse us in the mouth of a fool that would not amuse us in that of a gentleman; a fact which shows how little incongruity and degradation have to do with our pleasure in the comic. In fact, there is a kind of congruity and method even in fooling. The incongruous and the degraded displease us even there, as by their nature they must at all times [...] incongruity and degradation, as such, always remain unpleasant.[31]

---

31 George Satayana, *The Sense of Beauty* (New York: Scribner's, 1896) 249.

Objections of this kind are given more weight by theories of 'cognitive dissonance' like that argued by Leon Festinger (1919–1989): such theories suggest that human beings are driven to avoid the discomfort created by holding together two conflicting concepts (contagions) simultaneously; we find them upsetting, and so are invariably compelled to make adjustments to our thinking in order to achieve consonance. In short, our psychological need for consonance and reason are fundamentally at odds with Incongruity Theory.

5.6 So Where Does that Leave Us?

Pause and Reflect

Having identified incongruity in some of the jokes and humour that you are familiar with, try to detect ways in which the incongruity might be considered apt: why does that *particular* incongruity work while others may not? So, for instance, take this joke: '"Diner: Waiter there's a fly in my chicken soup." Waiter: "That's not a fly, that's the chicken."' The incongruity rests with the comparison between a fly and a chicken, but if you change fly to flea it would be just as incongruous yet not as funny. This is because the fly reference alludes to a well–known joke–form that begins 'Waiter there's a fly in my soup.' So fly is apposite where flea is not. Try to find similar evidence for appropriateness in other examples.

Some theorists have noted that while incongruity may be present in many instances of humour, incongruity is not in itself the source of amusement: rather, it is the resolution of the conflict that creates the humour and the pleasure. Incongruities that are not somehow resolved provide no pleasure. Neil Schaeffer, for instance, has written that:

> With incongruity we see two things which do not belong together, yet which we accept at least in this case as belonging together in some way. That is, when we notice something as incongruous, we also simultaneously understand it to be in some minor way congruous.[32]

---

32 Neil Schaeffer, *The Art of Laughter* (New York: Columbia University Press, 1981) 9.

This brings to mind Søren Kierkegaard's notion of the 'painless contradiction' and the idea of humorous incongruities offering a way out. The fact that comic incongruity is in some sense also 'congruous' circumvents the possibility of 'cognitive dissonance': it suggests a degree of resolution that renders it benign, and the irrationality of the incongruity does not disturb us the way it otherwise might.

Neil Schaeffer also stresses the importance of context in enabling the resolution of incongruities:

> I offer this definition: laughter results from an incongruity presented in a ludicrous context. That is, an incongruity, if it is to cause laughter, must be accompanied or preceded by a sufficient number of cues that indicate to an audience the risible intention of the incongruity and prepare them for the appropriate response of laughter. (Neil Schaeffer, *The Art of Laughter,* 17)

The 'cues' signal that what we are about to be presented with is meant to be seen as humorous, and this makes us more willing to suspend our insistence on reason and logic, thus creating a context in which incongruities are more readily resolvable. So, in the case of the New Jersey hunter joke, because the hunter's stupidity is presented within the frame of a joke (either by a comedian or in a joke book) we are willing to suspend our disbelief about the possibility of someone being so stupid.

The significance of incongruity–resolution in humour is discussed by Jerry Palmer in his book *Taking Humour Seriously* (1994). He cites the research of J. Suls who tested variations of the following joke on children:

1. 'Doctor, come at once! Our baby has swallowed a fountain pen!' 'I'll be right over. What are you doing in the meantime?' 'Using a pencil.'

2. 'Doctor, come at once! Our baby has swallowed a rubber band!' 'I'll be right over. What are you doing in the meantime?' 'Using a pencil.'

3. 'Doctor, come at once! Our baby has swallowed a foun-

tain pen!' 'I'll be right over. What are you doing in the meantime?' 'We don't know what to do.'[33]

Not surprisingly the children found the first version funnier than two and three. The third version has no incongruity: the parents' response, 'we don't know what to do,' is completely compatible with the idea of their child swallowing a fountain pen; there *is* an incongruity in the second, but this is not funny because there is no obvious relationship between swallowing a rubber band and using a pencil. The first version is the funny one, according the Suls, because here the incongruity is resolvable on one level: rather like the New Jersey hunter who shoots his friend to make sure he's dead, it is possible to imagine a scenario in which an idiot parent might mistake the doctor's medical question for a question about their stationary needs. Suls's incongruity–resolution theory suggests that amusement is created when we encounter an incongruity and then are compelled to resolve it with reference either to information provided in the joke, or our own knowledge of the world. Humour is absent until the incongruity is resolved, or until it is made to make sense in some way. Jerry Palmer himself calls this phenomenon 'the logic of the absurd,' in his own semiotic theory of humour. For Palmer jokes have a structure that involves two processes: firstly, 'The sudden creation of a discrepancy, or incongruity, in the joke narrative;' secondly, 'a bifurcated logical process, which leads the listener to judge that the state of affairs portrayed is simultaneously highly implausible and just a little bit plausible' (Jerry Palmer, *Taking Humour Seriously*, 96); the phrase 'just a little bit plausible' is crucial.

Theories claiming that humour depends on the resolution of incongruities are sometimes called Configurational Theories because of their focus on how incompatible concepts are configured in order to create amusement. Arguably, however, not all incongruities need to be resolved in order to have comic potential. By definition, examples of comic nonsense and absurdity cannot be resolved and yet remain a source of humour. Indeed, strictly speaking we could say that there is no such thing as 'logic of the absurd.' Consider this well–known

---

33 Cited in Jerry Palmer, *Taking Humour Seriously* (London: Routledge, 1994) 95–96.

nonsense piece by Christopher Isherwood:

> 'The Common Cormorant'
> The common cormorant or shag
> Lays eggs inside a paper bag.
> The reason you will see, no doubt,
> It is to keep the lightning out.
> But what these unobservant birds
> Have never noticed is that herds
> Of wandering bears may come with buns
> And steal the bags to hold the crumbs.[34]

Unlike some nonsense verse all the words here are real words strung together grammatically in a poem with a fairly predictable measure and rhyme scheme. The events it describes are incompatible with our experience of the world, however, and this incompatibility is a source of humour. There might be a sense in which such incongruities could be resolved at the level of metaphor by a literary critic, but the humour certainly does not depend on this. Some theorists would argue that this poem—and indeed nonsense in general— simply doesn't count as humour, at least for adults. The psychologist Thomas Schultz, for instance, claims that, 'after the age of seven, we require not just incongruity to be amused, but the resolution of that incongruity' (John Morreall, *A Comprehensive Philosophy of Humor*, 15). From my own perspective as a fifty one year old I think he is mistaken, and the fact that nonsense remains funny should make us want to think twice about accepting incongruity-resolution as applicable to all instances of humour.

Creative Writing Exercise

Have a go at writing a piece of nonsense verse: it's a good idea to begin with a poetic form such as a limerick. Here is an example from the famous exponent of nonsense verse, Edward Lear (1812–1888):

> There was an Old Man of the coast,
> Who placidly sat on a post;
> But when it was cold

---

34 Christopher Isherwood in *Poems Past and Present* (J. M. Dent and Sons, 1959).

He relinquished his hold
And called for some hot buttered toast.

Try to keep to the rhyme scheme and the rhythm, but introduce your own character, location and activity. Don't worry about it making sense, just attempt to make it funny. Is it possible to write an amusing limerick that is just pure nonsense?

6. Relief Theories

There are some similarities between Incongruity Theory and what is sometimes called Relief or Release Theory. The latter tend also to see laughter as born of contradictions, for instance, but they relocate that contradiction in the self rather than in the joke. Such theories are characterised by the notion that laughter involves the individual relieving pent–up energy, or letting–off steam.

6.1 Herbert Spencer: Nervous Energy

The British philosopher Herbert Spencer (1820–1903) is usually cited as the first person to formulate a relief theory of humour. He was particularly interested in finding ways to link nineteenth century scientific discoveries with philosophy, and his theory of humour draws heavily on the discourse of biology. Spencer is interested in how the perception of an incongruity becomes transformed into laughter. He thought that it is associated with the release of nervous energy, and he illustrates his theory quite succinctly with an example about a goat intruding on a love scene in at the theatre. It is worth quoting this in detail:

> You are sitting in a theatre, absorbed in the progress of an interesting drama. Some climax has been reached which has aroused your sympathies—say, a reconciliation between the hero and heroine, after long and painful misunderstanding [...] And now, while you are contemplating the reconciliation with a pleasurable sympathy, there appears from behind the scenes a tame kid, which, having stared round at the audience, walks up to the lovers and sniffs at them. You cannot help joining in the roar which greets this *contretemps* [...] it is readily explicable if we consider what, in such a case, must become of

the feeling that existed at the moment the incongruity arose. A large mass of emotion had been produced; or, to speak in physiological language, a large portion of the nervous system was in a state of tension. There was also great expectation with respect to the further evolution of the scene—a quantity of vague, nascent thought and emotion, into which the existing quantity of thought and emotion was about to pass. Had there been no interruption, the body of new ideas and feelings next excited, would have sufficed to absorb the whole of the liberated nervous energy. But now, this large amount of nervous energy, instead of being allowed to expend itself in producing an equivalent amount of the new thoughts and emotions which were nascent, is suddenly checked in its flow. The channels along which the discharge was about to take place, are closed. The new channel opened—that afforded by the appearance and proceedings of the kid—is a small one; the ideas and feelings suggested are not numerous and massive enough to carry off the nervous energy to be expended. The excess must therefore discharge itself in some other direction; and in the way already explained, there results an efflux through the motor nerves to various classes of the muscles, producing the half–convulsive actions we term laughter.[35]

The emotion produced by the drama creates tension within the nervous system of the spectator who had certain expectations about how the scene was going to develop: the build–up of tension was created by the anticipation of what he believed would happen next. The expectation is qualified, however, when a goat walks on to the scene, creating incongruity. The qualification means that the spectator no longer needs the nervous energy that had been created by the tension, and so that nervous energy is re–routed, and discarded in the form of laughter.

Spencer sought a physiological explanation for laughter, then, and his hydraulic energy model looks a little quaint in the twenty first century: his biological references seem rudimentary and naïve.

35 Herbert Spencer, 'The Physiology of Laughter,' *Macmillan's Magazine*, March 1860, 452–466 (461).

There are other problems with his theory too. For instance, laughter for Spencer is always a result of lowering our expectations, as with the bathetic image of the goat undermining the emotionally charged scene in his example; in other words his theory implies that laughter is always a consequence of descending incongruity, where something elevated is replaced by something trivial. His thesis doesn't really account for comic incongruities that work in the other direction, where something trivial is replaced by something of great consequence. There are many instances of the latter. One example might be the closing scenes of *The Simpsons* episode, *Fear of Flying*. In this episode Marge reveals that she has a fear of flying, and the show concludes with Homer, having finally coaxed her onto a plane, reassuring Marge that the various take–off sounds she can hear are perfectly normal; in the middle of his reassurances, however, the plane crashes into a swamp:

> **Homer**: Don't worry about a thing, honey. I'm going to help you through this.
> [He and Marge sit down; some noises occur]
> Those are all normal noises. Luggage compartment clos-ing...crosschecking...just sit back and relax.
> [Shot from outside the plane]
> That's just the engine powering up...that's just the engine struggling...
> [The plane drives off the runway into a swamp]
> That's just a carp swimming around your ankles...
> **Marge**: Mmm...[36]

Here incongruity is created between Homer's reassurances and the reality of plane crashing into a swamp, and laughter occurs at the point when the plane crashes. This would appear to be an example of ascending incongruity, where something trivial is replaced by some-thing massively significant. So how do the trivial, ostensibly insignif-icant reassurances of Homer build the tension necessary for a release

36 *Fear of Flying, Simpsons* Episode No 114, Writer., David Sacks., Director., Mark Kirkland, First broadcast November, 1994.

of nervous energy in Spencer's terms? Nevertheless we laugh. There *is* descending incongruity here too of course—but this comes *after* the plane has crashed into the swamp and Homer says, 'That's just a carp swimming around your ankles;' this is a brilliant comic under-statement that creates another potential laugh. Both the ascending incongruity and the descending incongruity are funny, but Spencer's theory only seems to work for one.

Creative Writing Exercise

> Create two comic scenes, one with descending incongruity where something elevated is replaced by something trivial, and one with ascending incongruity, where something trivial is replaced by something immensely significant. The former is easier, but the latter is possible.

6.2 Sigmund Freud: The Unconscious

There are problems with Spencer's theory, then, and it is of interest now principally in the extent to which it was adapted by Sigmund Freud (1856–1939). In *Jokes and Their Relation to the Unconscious* (1905), Freud takes Spencer's Relief Theory of laughter and reworks it in line with his own model of the human psyche and his view that laughter helps us release psychic energy, as opposed to nervous energy.

Freud addresses various causes of laughter and argues that all help regulate psychic energy. The reasons for the build–up and release of this psychic energy depend on the type of amusement. Laughter created when jokes address taboo subjects, for instance, constitutes a release of the energy that would otherwise have been used to repress those taboo feelings. Freud also argues that laughter occurs when comedy provides an escape from the demands of rational thought: the latter demands more psychic energy than comic irrationality, so jokes provide pleasure by offering freedom from the constraints of reason. Other causes of laughter can involve the release of energy caused when a seemingly serious situation turns out to be trivial (a view very similar to Spencer's notion of descending incongruity), or when more than one concept is combined in a single comic idea. In Freud's words, the pleasure that jokes produce, 'whether it is pleasure in play or pleasure in lifting inhibitions, can invariably be traced back to economy in physical expenditure.'[37] So like Spencer, Freud thought that humour helps us manage energy, but for him the mind is the source of this energy.

Freud made a distinction between 'innocent' jokes and 'tendentious' jokes; the latter are those which draw on taboos, and arguably it is Freud's discussion of this kind of joke that has been the most influential aspect of his work on humour. Andrew Stott, discussing Freud on this topic, explains his views in the following way:

> The need for [tendentious] jokes is a response to social expectations, as the norms of etiquette usually prevent us from directly insulting others or broaching taboo subjects. By touching on these difficult topics, the joke does important work, as it alleviates the inhibition of the joker and addresses the taboo while also keeping it in place. Laughing is the audible signal that the energy required for 'cathexis', the accumulation of energy around an idea, has been lifted and can now be dispersed in a pleasurable fashion. (Andrew Stott, *Comedy*, 139–140)

Taboo feelings—those relating to sex or violence and things that civilised society find unacceptable—are usually repressed; in other words they are kept in the unconscious. This repression requires psychic energy, but when we allow these topics into our conscious mind through joking we no longer require the energy we've been using to repress them: this superfluous energy is jettisoned in the form of laughter. Consider the following joke:

> A man boards a flight and finds himself seated next to a beautiful woman. They exchange brief hellos and he notices that she is reading a book. He asks her about it and she replies, 'It is a book about sexual statistics. It claims that American Indians have the longest average penis size of any men in the world,

---

37 Sigmund Freud, *Jokes and their Relation to the Unconscious* (London: Penguin Books, 1991) 189.

and Polish men's penises are the thickest in diameter. By the way, my name is Amanda. What's yours?' Without hesitation he replies, 'Tonto Kowalski, nice to meet you.'

Firstly, reflect on this joke in terms of what we know about incongruity. We can easily identify an incongruity and a resolution here: there is a discrepancy between what we expect the man to say at the end (a conventional name), and what he actually says (a name combining both of the 'well–endowed' ethnic groups). Also the incongruity is resolvable because the name, Tonto Kowalski, relates to and unites the statistics Amanda has referenced; plus it uses names which crudely connote the relevant ethnic groups: they are familiar enough to be what Jerry Palmer would call 'a little bit plausible'. It is also compatible with the way a man might try to impress a woman who he wants to get to know more intimately. Arguably, however, this incongruity–resolution feature is not enough to account for the full force of the humour. Imagine changing Amanda's book to one about wealth: the richest men are American Indians and the most generous are Poles. The punch line—Tonto Kowalski—would be just as incongruous, and the incongruity would be resolvable and plausible in a similar way, but it wouldn't be as funny as the original. Freud might argue that the original is funnier because it relates to sex, a taboo topic. For Freud, such tendentious jokes are inherently funnier than innocent jokes. The pleasure derived from an innocent joke does not have any real purpose or aim, and comes solely from the technique of the joke itself. For instance, in the innocent version of the Tonto Kowalski joke, the punch line would only be mildly amusing in Freud's scheme: it would still enable some saving of psychic energy because the two concepts of wealth and generosity are combined and contracted in the single idea of a man called Tonto Kowalski (it takes less energy to think about one thing than two things). However, this saving is meagre compared to the tendentious version. The latter is funnier because it has an ulterior motive: it is also acting as a vehicle for a desire that we are compelled to repress. As a result there is double the pleasure in the tendentious version: we enjoy the condensed punch line, but we also enjoy the lifting of inhibitions that the joke's subject permits.

In order to get a better sense of how Freud's theory of tendentious jokes applies here we need to create an audience. Imagine that the scene presented in the Tonto Kowalski joke is a real life situation in which Amanda isn't attracted to the man sitting next to her on the plane. For the man's Tonto Kowalski quip to work in Freud's terms there would need to be three people involved: the joke–teller, the butt (Amanda), and a third party audience. The joke–teller needs an audience because he does not save psychic energy simply by telling the joke: if this was possible then we would be able to tell jokes to ourselves, and laugh at them. The joke requires an audience because the audience's laughter validates the joke: they become complicit in the tampering with social codes, and thereby legitimise it for the teller. This sanction enables the release of energy; also, because laughter is infectious, the audience's laughter is likely to stimulate laughter in the joke–teller, and thus he can derive pleasure from his own joke.

Creative Writing Exercise

Consider the following joke:

> A psychiatrist was conducting a group therapy session with three young mothers and their small children. 'You all have obsessions,' he observed. To the first mother, he said, 'You are obsessed with eating. You've even named your daughter Candy.' He turned to the second mom. 'Your obsession is money; again it manifests itself in your child's name, Penny.' At this point the third mother got up, took her little boy by the hand and whispered, 'Come on, Dick, let's go.'

Try to write an innocent version of this joke. Start by experimenting with different obsessions and names for the children. When you have arrived at a version that you feel retains some humour, try to identify where the humour lies, and how Freud might account for it. Now have a go at writing another, different tendentious version. Change the mothers to fathers if that offers more possibilities. Did you find it easier to write a tendentious version, and was this version funnier?

6.3 Freud and Play

It was seen above how Schopenhauer saw a link between the pleasure of humour and the defeat of reason, and Freud's theory is similar in this sense. For Freud the pleasure to be derived from humour can lie in its ability to usurp rational thought; he felt that jokes recreate the pleasure of childhood play that adults lose as they mature. Consider these words from Peter L. Berger:

> Wit can be employed as a form of rebellion against authority. Most political jokes have this function. But Freud argues that there is a deeper rebellion; that against reason. This implies a kind of infantilization, a return to what Freud calls the 'old homestead' of childhood in which wishes come magically true and in which playing (including the play with words) makes up much of life. Joking is, in a way, becoming a child again for a few moments, and that in itself is a source of pleasure.[38]

To a degree, every example of humour can be viewed as an act of transgression against the authority reason, with the irrational world of humour offering temporary relief from the demands of the adult world. In this way it is also possible to account for the pleasure derived from the nonsense and absurdist humour discussed above. Freud's notion of psychic economy suggests that irrational thought requires less psychic energy than rational thought, and the excess finds a pleasurable release during childish humour. This pleasure is a guilty one because of the pressure the adult world exerts on us to toe–the–line and behave like grown–ups, but Freud suggests that jokes can offer a way of making such childishness acceptable in adult life; a joke can provide what might be termed a rational context for irra-tional behaviour, thereby legitimising conduct that would otherwise be unacceptable.

When you come to consider the vast amount of jokes that address taboos of various kinds, and the enduring appeal of childish humour, it is easy to see why Freud's argument might have some mileage. There are many problems with his ideas however. One difficulty with his theory of tendentious jokes, for instance, has to do with definition: it is often hard to distinguish them from innocent jokes.

---

38 Peter L. Berger. *Redeeming Laughter: The Comic Dimension of Human Experience* (Berlin: Walter de Gruyter & Co, 1997), 56.

For one thing, whether or not a joke would be deemed offensive/taboo must depend partly on interpretation. Also Freud's theory seems to imply that the more taboo a subject, the funnier it will be, but this is not necessarily the case. Most comedians are aware of the concept of crossing the line with a joke, and if a joke addresses a taboo of sufficient magnitude then it's likely to create outrage rather than laughter. However, the problems with Freud's theory are more fundamental that this: the main issue has to do with the crucial fact that his hydraulic model of the psyche, with its economy of psychic energy, is simply not provable.

Pause and Reflect

Consider some of the ways in which humour can be rebellious. How might humour work to challenge authority, and what examples of this can you identify?

6.4 Mikhail Bakhtin: Carnival

> 'Against the assault of humour nothing can stand.'
> —Mark Twain.

Despite the weaknesses of Freud's theory, he has had a huge influence on those who strive to theorise humour. This is particularly so for people interested in the relationship between humour and authority, and the ways humour might help us live with authority by acting as a safety valve. Some suggest that humour is essential for enabling people to let of steam, and maintaining the status quo. Certainly at a psychological level Freud felt that jokes play a part in upholding psychological equilibrium:

> the euphoria which we endeavour to reach by these means is nothing other than the mood of a period of life in which we were accustomed to deal with our psychical work in general with a small expenditure of energy—the mood of our childhood, when we were ignorant of the comic, when we were incapable of jokes and when we had no need of humour to make us feel happy in our life (Freud, *Jokes*, 302).

For Freud, joking becomes a way of returning us to childhood and relieving us temporarily of the burden of adulthood; in other words, joking serves a useful function because such relief keeps us in psychological health. In this sense, parallels can be drawn between Freud's thinking and that of the Russian philosopher and literary critic, Mikhail Bakhtin (1895–1975). In his book, *Rabelais and His World* (1941), Bakhtin developed the concept of carnival and the carnivalesque, which has been very influential, particularly among literary critics. He discusses the characteristics and social function of medieval carnivals such as the Feast of Fools. In catholic countries like France and Spain feasts of this kind were associated with a period of revelry that precedes Lent: the big party before the fasting. Bakhtin noted that carnivals featured behaviour that would otherwise be socially unacceptable, allowing ordinary people to mock figures of authority: dignitaries could be parodied, including the clergy and the monarchy. Standard codes, conventions and laws could be suspended for the period of the celebration, and carnivals effectively turned the traditional social hierarchy on its head.

The humour found in carnivals is characterised by grotesquery, scatology (toilet humour), anti–intellectualism, colloquialism, an emphasis on the body, and general excess: it is a form of humour that works against all notions of authority, including the authority of reason, taste, and piety. Carnival humour is very much the people's humour in that it proclaims the voice of the ordinary folk in opposition to the powers–that–be. Here is Bakhtin discussing the dissenting spirit of carnival:

> one might say that carnival celebrated temporary liberation from the prevailing truth and from the established order; it marked the suspension of all hierarchical rank, privileges, norms and prohibitions. Carnival was the true feast of time, the feast of becoming, change and renewal. It was hostile to all that was immortalized and completed.[39]

Voices that are normally supressed by authority have full reign during

---

39 Mikhail Bahktin. *Rabelais and His World*. Trans, Helene Iswolsky (Cambridge, MA:MIT Press, 1984) 10.

the carnival period, and we can see how this relates to the notion of letting off steam through laughter. Where Freud's theory deals with the benefits of humour for the individual psyche, Bakhtin is interested in how this worked in social terms, and the ability of carnival to function as a social safety valve. Bakhtin was not particularly concerned with modern carnivals like contemporary *Mardi Gras* as these are more like spectator events where people watch a procession of other people, without being truly involved. For him a true carnival is one where people play an active part: an opportunity for ordinary people go out on the streets and assert their collective identity and values:

> The carnivalesque crowd in the marketplace or in the streets is not merely a crowd. It is the people as a whole, but organized in their own way, the way of the people. It is outside of and contrary to all existing forms of the coercive socioeconomic and political organization, which is suspended for the time of the festivity. (Bahktin, *Rabelais*, 255)

Bakhtin was very interested in how the spirit of carnival registers in literature, and as the title of his book suggests, he focussed principally on the French writer Rabelais (1494–1553), whose work was full of carnival humour. For Bakhtin, carnivalised texts can challenge the controlling, dominant voice of authority by juxtaposing the high culture that represents that authority, with the earthy, base comedy of carnival. In this way texts have the potential to become sites of opposition to the dominant ideology.

Pause and Reflect

Can you think of any examples of carnivalesque comedy in modern humour? What form does it take, and in what sense does it challenge authority?

It is possible to find elements of carnival humour in many texts, including modern popular comedy. Again *The Simpsons* might serve as an example. The show is full of grotesques (Barney, Homer, Mo), and it teems with low humour. Homer and Bart both exhibit carnival characteristics: they're both anti–intellectual, for instance, going out of their way to be unsophisticated, and both challenge authority in numerous ways: Bart is in conflict with his teachers, and with his sister Lisa and her status as a model child. He defies the codes of behaviour that she embodies, just for the sake of it. Likewise Homer rebels against all that his neighbour Ned Flanders represents; Homer hates him even though there's no obvious reason to. In many respects Flanders is the perfect neighbour, but that's exactly why Homer dislikes him; he embodies a standard that he himself can't match. Homer's carnival humour challenges the authority of that standard. Homer is at his most extreme and disgusting (and morally dubious) when he's trying to get one over on Flanders. Often this takes the form of him trying to reduce Ned to his own level: in one episode, for instance, Homer takes Ned to Las Vegas, gets him drunk, and married to a hooker; in another he tries to ruin his business. Homer does disgraceful things—but carnival is happy to be disgraceful; there are no limits to which it will go in order to debase, deflate, undermine, challenge, and ridicule. While the viewers may feel that Ned is in the right morally, it's Homer who most people are behind on an emotional level, chiefly because Homer's dissent is funny. However, it is notable that in most *Simpsons* stories Homer eventually gets his comeuppance in some way: his wife Marge will make him feel ashamed of himself, for instance, or he'll be publicly humiliated. This is important because, while the rebellion and disorder associated with carnival is attractive, it is also anti–social. As much as people may like it, they are also wary of it. They may be temporarily drawn to the lack of responsibility associated with carnival, but they wouldn't want it to last because disorder and chaos are incompatible with social stability. So after the carnival everything returns to normal again, and the status quo is re–established. When carnival becomes a feature of literature or popular narratives you often find that it's countered in this way: there's frequently a qualifying force that reins it in. Society is nothing without order, structure, even hierarchy. So just like real carnivals, the carnival spirit in narrative frequently deals in transient relief, ending with a reestablishment of the status quo.

Creative Writing Exercise

Create a character who does everything to excess, but doesn't care. Try imagining them in different situations where restraint and decorum are demanded (Churches, restaurants, museums, etc.). A wealth of comic possibilities should suddenly present themselves. As you experiment you may happen upon interesting ideological pressures and prejudices that can be exposed via your carnival character. For instance, imagine a character that eats to excess in a context where it is unseemly to gorge oneself: this has comic potential, of course, but notice how the implications of such behaviour will differ if you changed the gender of the character.

7. Humour and Ethics

If humour has beneficial social and psychological functions, then we might assume that it is a necessary part of our lives. However, given its association with superiority and taboo, humour can be socially oppressive and offensive, and this raises difficult ethical questions. How do we square our apparent need for humour with our social responsibilities? The issue of the morality of humour has been addressed by philosophers throughout the ages, and this section will examine the key areas of debate.

Pause and Reflect

In social terms, is humour always a positive thing? List some of the good and bad things that might be associated with humour and laughter.

7.1 John Morreall: On the Positive and Negative Ethics of Humour

In his book *Comic Relief* (2009), John Morreall discusses what he terms the positive and a negative ethics of humour, offering a–for–and–against debate about the morality of humour. Beginning with the negative aspects of humour, he lists various reasons why we might object to humour on moral grounds. Firstly humour is associated with lies: when we joke we take liberties with the truth, and duplicity and dissimulation often feature in humour. We value authenticity in our communications, and because we are wary when this is undermined, we may object to humour on these grounds. Also, we saw in our discussion of Freud and Bakhtin that humour is associated with play, but this too can have a negative dimension. When we are at play we are not working: we are engaged in something that is other than productive. So in this sense humour is linked to idleness, which is generally thought to be bad. Play can also be self–indulgent and hedonistic, of course, and humour is potentially problematic in this respect too. Also, as laughter is associated with physical pleasure, it has often been frowned upon in societies where pleasure and the desires of the body are deemed sinful or distracting. For instance, Morreall notes laughter's long association with a lack of sexual restraint in woman; indeed it is still a sign of promiscuity if a woman laughs with her mouth open in certain Asian countries. Humour also has connotations irresponsibility, and some have objected to it on these grounds. The objections here are most evident perhaps when someone is being laughed at. There is a famous quote by Mel Brooks in which he distinguishes between tragedy and comedy: 'Tragedy is when I cut my finger. Comedy is when you fall into an open sewer and die.' Most people will recognise a degree of validity in this statement, and it doesn't reflect well on comedy. In other words there is an extent to which humour might encourage us to disengage from other people and have detrimental social consequences as a result: we saw earlier how it can be used to block emotions. In Morreall's terms, humour 'can cause harm by blocking compassion for those who need help,' (John Morreall, *Comic Relief*, 103). Humour and laughter can be nasty, then, and a host of philosophers from Plato onwards have been suspicious of it for this reason. While we know that we shouldn't laugh when someone falls into an open sewer and dies, some fear that cultivating a fondness for laughter might encourage callousness of this kind.

Obviously it is easy to defend humour from some of these accusations. Firstly, while acknowledging that humour and laughter can have all these negative features, it is simple to think of humorous situations where none of them apply. Also, some of the criticism levelled against humour seems equally applicable to other perfectly acceptable activities. For instance, while fabrication and insincerity may well be a feature of humour, it is also a feature of fiction and drama. It is worth noting here perhaps that, from a psychological perspective, those who find it hard to tolerate lapses from literal facts tend not to have a sense of humour. Victor Raskin has suggested that: 'truthfulness—a commitment to the literal truth of what is said under any circumstances and in any mode of communication—should be seen as counterindicative of the sense of humor.'[40] Humour depends on an understanding that comic lapses from the truth have a different status from lying. Also, while humour might be associated with pointless and potentially self–indulgent entertainment, couldn't the same be said of the arts in general? With respect to the issue of the possible irresponsibility of humour, it is worth noting that most people *wouldn't* laugh if they *literally* saw someone fall into an open sewer and die. Brooks' quip makes a valid point about the occasional relationship between humour and *schadenfreude*, but he is exaggerating for comic effect. When we laugh at that quip we laugh at the hyperbole; in other words, we laugh partly because it distorts reality. It's the perfect example of a comic incongruity in that it's both false and a little bit true. Of course the extent to which it is false is critical: humour might be able to block compassion to a degree, but it is hard to imagine it doing so completely. Thus we might be able to find humour in a fictional (comic) representation of someone falling into an open sewer and dying, but in reality this would more likely cause horror. So for most people there is a point at which another's misfortune would destroy rather than increase the potential for laughter.

So what are the ethically sound aspects of humour? According to Morreall humour has the potential to promote both intellectual and moral virtues. From an intellectual perspective, for instance, the psychological research of people like Alice Isen and Avner Ziv shows that humour can stimulate original and creative thinking:

> Humour promotes divergent thinking in two ways. First, it blocks negative emotions such as fear, anger, and sadness, which suppress creativity by steering thought into familiar channels. Secondly, humour is a way of appreciating cognitive shifts: when we are in a humorous frame of mind, we are automatically on the lookout for unusual ideas and new ways

---

40 Victor Raskin, 'The Sense of Humor and the Truth. In W. Ruch, ed., *The Sense of Humor: Explorations of a Personality Characteristic* (Berlin/New York: Mouton de Gruyter) 95–108 (108).

of putting things together. (John Morreall, *Comic Relief*, 113)

Humour can help us shake ourselves free of conventional thought processes: we become more receptive to alternative ways of thinking when we are in a humorous mode, and this has potentially positive social and psychological consequences. When we are in a humorous mode we are also more adept at thinking critically. When thinking humorously we are more aware of incongruities, and this may extend to disparities between appearance and reality. In the social sphere, Morreall argues, this may boost our capacity to discern hypocrisy and deceit, making us more likely to challenge rather than acquiesce to the powers–that–be: 'we are not likely to blindly follow leaders, or do something merely because "we've always done it this way"' (John Morreall, *Comic Relief*, 113).

Humour is linked to moral virtues too, and for Morreall this has to do with its ability to affect 'self–transcendence.' In other words humour can enable us to step outside ourselves and gain a less egocentric perspective than might otherwise be available. Society tends to see the ability to laugh at oneself, and not to take oneself too seriously as a positive trait. People who cannot do this are often seen as self–important or self–obsessed. Self–deprecating humour is good because it suggests humility. Morreall argues too that a sense of humour is conducive to tolerance and patience: framing bad news or information in a humorous way can offset its negative impact. The tradition of the court jester is worth noting here: in the past humour gave a jester licence to communicate unpalatable truths to the king. Imagine a skilful jester encouraging a stubborn king to laugh at himself, and you can see how acceptance, lenience and broadmindedness are all virtues that might be fostered by humour. Humour can offer a means of solidarity for people too, and this is often the case during times of oppression. The most often cited example is that of Jewish humour. The Jews have a history of oppression, and humour is felt to have functioned as a coping mechanism for them at times of extreme crisis; it has worked to offset adversity, most notably during the Holocaust. For instance Morreall cites examples of joking about the dearth of food in the Lodz ghetto: 'Before the war we ate ducks and walked like horses; now we eat horses and walk like ducks' (Morreall, *Comic Relief*, 123). This 'coping humour' has a positive function both for the individual and for the oppressed community as a whole.

For Morreall, the positive outweighs the negative when it comes to the ethics of humour. He associates the cultivation of humour with wisdom, and the ability to live well. Indeed he argues that humour can help us acquire essential knowledge for living well: we can, for instance, learn how to avoid behaviour that would turn us into the butts of jokes; we can learn to critically assess institutions which claim authority over our lives; we can learn to privilege humour over violence; we can learn to enjoy life, and take pleasure in its absurdities rather than let them traumatise or annoy us; we can learn to disengage from life, when appropriate, and achieve a more objective perspective; not least, we can learn how to use humour to bond with like–minded individuals.

Creative Writing Exercise

> This exercise concerns adopting the kind of 'humorous frame of mind' that might be conducive to creativity. Those people with a natural feel for humour will find it easier than others, but there are techniques that can help. As with some of the other creative exercises, this is best done with a friend. Try to find an example of a comedy that you both agree is funny (a comic film, sit com, etc.). Using the existing characters, try to write a new story for them. So, for instance, if you're both fans of a particular sit com, plan an original script for the show. If you have any kind of rapport with your friend then you'll find yourselves in a humorous mode quickly enough. As your confidence develops, start trying to be more inventive. Introduce new characters into this comic world. If these new characters have the potential to carry a story of their own, then start writing it. This is a way of using someone else's work both as a means of creating an appropriate mind-set for humour, and as the springboard for original comic ideas.

7.2 Ethnic Humour

While humour can offer a route to social solidarity and bonding, it can also be divisive. When communities bond through humour, it is often at the expense of another community; for this reason much discussion of the ethics of humour has focussed on ethnic and sexist humour—in other words humour that seems to privilege one group over another.

7.3 Christie Davis

Before going on to discuss the ethical issues raised by racist and sexist jokes, it is worth saying something about what they are and how they function. One of the leading authorities on ethnic jokes is Christie Davis, who discusses them from a sociological perspective in books such as *Ethnic Humor Around the World* (1990) and *Jokes and Targets* (2011). The most common form of ethnic jokes is stupid–ethnic jokes, where a member of an ethnic minority is cast in the role of an idiot. Alongside these, and almost as prevalent, are what are often referred to as canny–ethnic jokes. Canny means shrewd, but it also means calculating, stingy, and crafty. So it's the opposite of stupid, in a sense, but it's not a compliment. In canny ethnic jokes, canny people are presented as astute, but they're also devious, sly, underhand and mean. In a given society a particular social group will be labelled dim, while another social group will be labelled canny. For instance, in Britain, Irish people are the butt of stupid jokes, Scottish are the butt of canny jokes; in America, Polish people are the butt of stupid jokes, Jews are the butt of canny jokes; in Italy, Southern Italians are stupid, Milanese and Florentines are canny, and so on. There are various historical social reasons why certain groups get labelled stupid or canny, but it is generally just an accident of history with no basis in reality. So what function do such jokes serve? According to Davis:

> Ethnic jokes about stupidity inevitably flourish in modern societies based on competition, rational calculation, and technical innovation, for stupidity means failure and the downfall of self and others alike.[41]

We live in a competitive world and the only way we can flourish is if

41 Christie Davis, *Ethnic Humor Around the World* (Indiana: Indiana University Press, 1990) 28.

we have the intellectual ability to compete, so we fear being seen as stupid. The message of stupid ethnic jokes is that *our* community is clever, compared to the others. So they convey a heartening message. Our world is deeply flawed and human stupidity is often perceived as contributing to that. If there weren't so many stupid people around, then the world would be a better place! Again, the message that jokes convey is that it's the other group, and not us who are the problem. As Davis says, the 'reassuring humorous message for joke tellers is [the butt of the joke]—and they alone—are comically stupid. We are not them. Therefore we are not stupid.' Likewise, people tell canny jokes because canniness is also something we fear in ourselves. While modern society encourages us to be successful—particularly financially successful—on the one hand, it also encourages us to be sociable and generous, on the other. Canny people aren't sociable and generous because they put too much emphasis on financial success at the expense of others. Not only is the world being ruined by dumb people, then, it's also being ruined by canny people: by greedy, self-ish, devious people. In other words, Davis argues that canny–ethnic jokes address a similar unease about failure: something else that we fear in ourselves that we project onto others.

Ethnic jokes are pervasive, then, and they would seem to have a social and psychological function. The degree to which they are deemed socially acceptable depends on the social context, but they always have the potential to offend, and to be labelled racist. Many people still find them funny, of course, even though they might feel guilty about laughing at them. How might we assess them on a moral level?

Pause and Reflect

Could there ever be a case for censoring humour? If so, how would this work and how would such censorship be enforced?

7.4 Walsall People Are Stupid

The town of Walsall in the English West Midlands is often mocked, particularly in regional culture for being an ugly town; also its townsfolk are occasionally labelled as stupid in the manner of a disparaged minority. For example:

> Did you hear the one about the dead Walsall bloke in the cupboard? He was last year's hide and seek winner.

> Why shouldn't Walsall workers be given coffee breaks?
> It takes too long to retrain them.

I was born in Walsall and I think this gives me some licence to make jokes of this kind, but would anyone have legitimate grounds to be offended by them? Perhaps if I wrote a social–history of Walsall asserting that Walsall people can't be given coffee breaks because it takes too long to retrain them, and I couldn't prove that this was true, people would have cause to be offended. In this case I would be misrepresenting facts in a context where we expect truth. Similarly if I were to make such claims in a piece of journalism, or in a political manifesto, then again people might legitimately complain: in these contexts we'd want the claims to be based on facts established by research. However, as we have seen, jokes aren't a context in which we expect the truth; rather they're a context in which we expect people to be joking. Jokes, by definition, don't make truth claims. They create a world in which everything is potentially false, where everything potentially undermines itself. So we're not supposed to take them literally. To take jokes literally is not to have a sense of humour. Also most people understand that to cast a group as stupid in a joke does not mean that they really are stupid. The Walsall jokes cited above are variations of blonde jokes, and it's clearly not the case that all blondes are stupid. In one sense the truth status of these claims is irrelevant anyway because a joke does not need to be true in order to be funny. For instance, an Incongruity Theorist might argue that what we laugh at in such jokes is the structure of the joke. The narrative sets up certain expectations, and then undermines them, and it is the sudden shift in logic, the sudden incongruity, that makes us laugh. If we laugh at Walsall stupidity in a joke, we are not laughing because we think that it is true—we have no way of knowing if it is or not. We're not laughing at reality, we're laughing an incongruity.

However there are people who argue that we relate to such jokes at a deep psychological level, and that laughing at them is never innocent. One contemporary philosopher, Ronald De Sousa, for instance, claims that to find such jokes funny is morally objectionable because it means that one shares their views; he argues that such jokes depend on one adopting an 'attitude' toward the disparaged group, and such an 'attitude' is effectively the same as a belief: 'attitudes are beliefs that one cannot hypothetically adopt,' and as a result it is impossible to be morally disengaged from the attitude expressed: to laugh at it is to share it, at least on one level.[42] De Sousa cites a sexist joke about rape and claims that anyone who finds it funny shares its sexist attitudes; he doesn't believe that it's possible to engage with it on a purely imaginative level. This view has been effectively countered by many commentators, however, including Berys Gaut, who makes the point that:

> I can imagine what it is like to adopt the attitudes character-istic of a desperate person, a Republican, or a maniac, and I can do that because imagination in these cases minimally involves the non–doxastic representation of the attitudes con-cerned, and such representation is clearly possible. Moreover, merely imagining an attitude may in some cases be all that is necessary to find a joke funny [...] I can hold to be funny jokes told by Jews about themselves, even though as a non–Jew I cannot share the self–directed attitudes on which they depend for their self–deprecatory humour.[43]

So Gaut argues that imagination is all that is required to find such jokes funny; it is not necessary to share the attitudes to which the joke appeals. From this we could conclude that if you laugh at an offen-sive joke you need not necessarily feel guilty about it. So don't worry about being Walsallist.

Some argue that if offensive jokes make no claims to truth, and don't depend on reality for their humour, they need not be considered

---

42 Ronald De Sousa, 'When is it Wrong to Laugh?' in John Morreall, ed., *The Philosophy of Laughter* (New York: State University of New York Press, 1987) 241.

43 Berys Gaut, 'Just Joking: The Ethics and Aesthetics of Humor,' *Philosophy and Literature*, 22, 1998 (51–68) 57.

morally objectionable. It could be said, for instance, that true racist discourse is markedly different from joking because true racist discourse *does* make claims to reality; genuine racist discourse does construct itself as the truth. The speeches of Adolf Hitler were racist because they claimed to be underpinned by truth. If we concede that jokes only exist in order to be funny, then how can they be racist? Consider these words from the British comic novelist Howard Jacobson:

> Once we accept that a joke is a structured dialogue with itself, that it cannot, by its nature, be an expression of opinion, you have conceded its unlikeness to racist discourse, which by its nature is impermeable and cannot abide contradiction.[44]

Pause and Reflect

Howard Jacobson's view is that jokes do not have opinions, and they undermine themselves as narratives: does this make you feel more comfortable about racist jokes? If not, why?

You can quote views like Jacobson's in perpetuity but they don't make people any more comfortable with racist jokes. The problem with them becomes more evident if we substitute Walsall for Irish in the example above. This makes us feel more uncomfortable about the joke because, while such jokes might not be interested in truth, or in expressing an opinion, they *do* utilize and perpetuate stereotypes. We know that stereotypes are potentially undesirable because they are reductive: whether a stereotype is positive or negative it reduces a group of people to a single characteristic and to do so is to diminish, and possibly dehumanise them. This may not be too much of a problem for Walsall people because they aren't a vulnerable minority; they aren't discriminated against socially. If we substitute Walsall for Irish it might be more of a problem because the history of British colonialism is such that the Irish have been presented as subordinate in English culture. There has been a perceived hierarchy in the historical relationship between England and Ireland that stupid Irishmen

44 Howard Jacobson, *Seriously Funny* (London: Channel Four Books, 1997) 36.

jokes might be said to reinforce. Irish people aren't a particularly vulnerable group and you still hear Irish jokes in popular culture, but the more discriminated against the ethnic minority, the less comfortable most people will be at making jokes at their expense. Imagine substituting Walsall for Black. Black people both in the UK and America have a long history of discrimination, of course, and negative stereotyping has played a huge part in this. Joseph Boskin, for instance, has written about the negative stereotyping of African Americans in humour. He draws on the ideas of Henri Bergson to make a point about the 'duplicating nature' of humour: according to Bergson, when something is reproduced often enough in a comic context, 'it reaches the state of being a classical type or model. It becomes amusing in itself, quite apart from the causes that render it amusing.'[45] Boskin argues that the derogatory stereotype of the Sambo is an example of this transformation from flesh and blood individuals into a 'comic machine–person':

> The Sambo stereotype, whose longevity reflected its deeply rooted functions, was an essential form of hostile humour. Sambo was Bergson's comic 'machine–person,' the palpable absurdity, subscribed to by whites in their attempt to preserve social distance between themselves and blacks, to maintain a sense of racial superiority and to prolong the class structure. The stereotyping of the black as one of the major comics in the popular culture of the United States is an example of psychological and cultural reduction. Sambo, then, illustrates the unique historical relationship between stereotyping and humouring. (Joseph Boskin, 'The Complicity of Humor,' 261–262)

We might disapprove of disparaging ethnic jokes because they deal in negative stereotypes, then, and because they can be reactionary; they can reinforce social structures which are unjust and discriminatory, buttressing social prejudices. While it may well be possible to partake of ethnic humour *without* being racist, there is no doubt that some advocates of racist humour *are* racist; and while it might be pos-

45 Joseph Boskin, 'The Complicity of Humor: The Life and Death of Sambo,' in John Morreall, ed., *The Philosophy of Laughter* (New York: State University of New York Press, 1987) 257.

sible to engage with such jokes on a detached, imaginative level, it is certainly the case that some people genuinely accept negative representations of ethnic groups as reality. Also Freud's theories would suggest that the fact that some people find such jokes upsetting is exactly the reason other people enjoy telling them: for Freud humour can have an aggressive function precisely because it is associated with the fulfilment of supressed desires; it can be a socially acceptable form of hostility. One of the implications of Freud's theory is that people find some jokes pleasurable *because* they are cruel.

As we have seen, Superiority Theorists argue that we laugh when our sense of superiority is confirmed. We laugh at perceived flaws in others, and in much ethnic humour, particularly in stupid–ethnic jokes, people who have power are laughing at people who, because they're outside the dominant social group, *don't* have power. The same is true of sexist jokes which belittle women and thus reinforce patriarchy, an unequal social structure where men have power at the expense of women's freedoms and right to parity. As some see it, then, humour can be a powerful factor in reinforcing social hierarchies, diminishing social groups, and as such has a negative effect on the community. This is why we might want to disapprove of racist and sexist jokes.

So what should we do about it? Should jokes of this kind be outlawed? There are comedians who make a living out of telling them on both sides of the Atlantic: should society censor overtly racist/ sexist comedians like Chubby Brown in the UK or Andrew Dice Clay in America? That would be hard for a variety of reasons. If Freud is correct, for instance, wouldn't social censorship only augment their taboo status, potentially making them funnier? Also, more importantly, to censor joke narratives is to censor something that, as we've seen, isn't *inherently* racist. If you allow that a narrative is articulating a joke, rather than a fact, then in a manner of speaking it can't be. This is essentially the view of the American philosopher Ted Cohen, whose reflections on jokes will be discussed below.

Creative Writing Exercise

Imagine that a stand–up comedian delivers an offensive routine on national television about your gender, ethnic group or sexual orientation. Think about what you might find offensive in such a routine then write an imaginary letter to that comedian explaining why they should change the nature of their material. Begin your letter, Dear 'Comedian.'

7.5 Ted Cohen: Just Joking

Ted Cohen's book, *Jokes: Philosophical Thoughts on Joking Matters* (1999) is exclusively about jokes, but his conclusions are relevant to many general situations in which humour and laughter occur. He concedes that there are things we should be wary of joking about, and feels that joking can become a form of avoidance. Some things in life need to be addressed without humour, and if we're not careful humour can work to deflect us from issues and experiences that should be confronted. He quotes Mark Twain's famous line, 'Against the assault of humour nothing can stand,' but makes the point that 'there are some things that should remain standing.'[46] A subject such as death is often the focus of humour, for instance, but while comedy may offer a valid and helpful response to this in certain contexts, it 'cannot be the entire human response' to such issues. A reaction to death that is exclusively humorous is lacking in something important, and may indeed be a way of avoiding the reality of the event. At the same time a response to death—or indeed to anything—that does not 'include the possibility of jokes is less than a totally human response' (Cohen, *Jokes*, 70). Joking is fundamental to the human condition for Cohen, then, and its significance—while it shouldn't necessarily be privileged—should never be ignored or supressed. It is this belief that informs his thinking on the morality of joking.

Cohen allows that some jokes can be tasteless and offensive, and as such they should be deemed objectionable; however, the problem with establishing grounds for making moral judgements about them has to do with their status as fictions. In the case of an offensive ethnic joke, there may well be some people who interpret it as true—those who are prejudiced against Walsall folks, for instance, might

---

46 Ted Cohen, *Jokes: Philosophical Thoughts on Joking Matters* (Chicago: Chicago University Press, 1999) 70.

genuinely believe in their inferiority; but the joke itself cannot be condemned a result: as suggested earlier, it makes no sense to condemn something that does not have opinions. Cohen admits to being simultaneously amused and disturbed by disparaging ethnic jokes that deal in reductive stereotypes, but does not believe it is possible to establish a moral theory that would allow us to judge them as immoral. To make his point he invokes a tool occasionally employed in conceptual moral theory: the notion of an ideal observer. Cohen invites us to imagine an observer who is completely objective and infinitely wise, and then ask how such an observer would respond to a disparaging ethnic joke. With laughter? With guilty laughter? With outrage? With condemnation? Most people would agree that it is impossible to say. However, this does not mean that people's outrage at such jokes is invalid—just as jokes cannot be condemned with reference to any single moral theory, they cannot be defended either. People who are offended by a particular joke have a right to say so, but they should be wary of claiming that such objectionable jokes are never funny. Cohen states that:

> the offended person who takes issue with a joke finds himself doubly assaulted, first by the offensive portrayal in the joke, and then again by the implicit accusation that he is humour-less. But the offended person may make the reflexive mistake of denying that the joke is funny. More than once someone has demanded of me that I explain exactly why anti–Semitic jokes are not funny. I have come to realise that if there is a problem with such jokes, the problem is compounded exactly by the fact that they *are* funny. Face that fact. And then let us talk about it. (Cohen, *Jokes*, 83–4)

For Cohen, to claim that an ethnic joke is not funny just because it is upsetting is an indication of cowardice and denial that cannot change the principal problem, which is: people have negative feelings about other social groups. His advice is not to deny that such jokes are funny, but to focus instead on determining why they are.

As suggested, Cohen sees joking and the appreciation of humour as a fundamentally human trait, and like Morreall he views humour's capacity to affect solidarity between people as a positive aspect of joking. That this solidarity is often expressed in opposition to or at the expense of another group doesn't diminish the significance and potential of this phenomenon. When we share jokes we are reaching out to others, partly, Cohen says because:

> I need reassurance that this something inside me, the something that is tickled by a joke, is indeed something that constitutes an element of my humanity. I discover something of what it is to be a human being by finding this thing in me, and then having it echoed in you, another human being. (Cohen, *Jokes*, 31)

Cohen asks the reader to imagine a world where no one finds the same things funny; it is indeed a useful exercise to do this, and I think most people would be chilled by the prospect of a world in which it was impossible to share humour. It underscores the extent that humour and laughter are social activities, and adds weight to Cohen's view that they are fundamentally linked to our sense of humanity.

Creative Writing Exercise

> Write a short story in which a character with a humorous disposition wakes up one morning to discover that he is living in a world in which everyone else is lacking a sense of humour.

8. Humour and Religion

Pause and Reflect

Can you think of any objections that religions or religious people might have to humour?

Humour and laughter might appear to be removed from the question of morality—this is the implication of Howard Jacobson's view as we've seen. Though they have moral consequences, humour and laughter sometimes look amoral. As Vassilis Saroglou has written, 'humour seems to be located in an area beyond the distinction of good and evil: it implies an "arrest of moral judgment."'[47] This may be one of the reasons why there has been such an uneasy relationship between religion and humour over the years. Indeed, according to Saroglou, there is strong evidence for suggesting that religion and humour are incompatible, certainly in a psychological sense: in his view a strongly religious disposition seems to be at odds with a sense of humour. For one thing a religious temperament suggests a desire for meaning, and a tendency to privilege unity and integration. By contrast humour—particularly absurdist humour—can challenge meaning and undermine unity. To make his point Saroglou cites Milan Kundera's excellent distinction between tragedy and comedy:

> By providing us with the lovely illusion of human greatness, the tragic brings us consolation. The comic is crueller: it brutally reveals the meaninglessness of everything.[48]

---

47 Vassilis Saroglou, 'Religion and Sense of Humor: An A Priori Incompatibility? Theoretical Considerations from a Psychological Perspective,' *Humor* 15–2 (2002), 191–214.

48 Milan Kundera, *The Art of the Novel*, Translated by L. Asher (London: Faber and Faber, 1988) 126.

Comedy's association with meaninglessness is at odds with religion's desire for meaning. In this sense religion is at odds with philosophy too: traditionally the latter is about asking questions, while the former assumes it knows the answers! Also, as we have seen, humour is born of incongruity and ambiguity, qualities which allow it to challenge norms and conventional ways of thinking; this may be another reason for incompatibility between humour and religion: the latter is inclined toward conservative thinking, and can rarely tolerate dissent from sacred narratives:

> It seems reasonable to suspect that religion may not be attracted to a celebration of incongruity, ambiguity and, most importantly, possibility of nonsense. In more strictly cognitive terms, one may hypothesize that the perception, or at least enjoyment, of incongruity is not encouraged by religion .(Vassilis Saroglou, 'Religion and Sense of Humor,' 195)

Also religions tend to privilege security and reliability, and therefore the element of experimentation often found in humour can be unsettling for people of a religious disposition. Religions are underpinned by predictability whereas humour depends on surprise. Humour's associations with unproductive play, hedonism and self–indulgence also sit uneasily with religion, as do its links to taboo topics like sex and aggression. Humour is at odds with literal truth too, of course, while religions tend to see lapses from truth as morally dubious.

However, while Saroglou's argument seems to suggest that humour and religion appeal to different kinds of thinking, humour can play a part in religion, and this section will go on to consider some of the ways in which humour features in three of the world's great religions.

8.1 Humour and Christianity

Early Christianity has a history of being critical of humour and laughter. The Bible makes several negative references to both, including famously in The Book of Ecclesiastes, purportedly written by Solomon:

> Sorrow is better than laughter: for by the sadness of the coun-

tenance the heart is made better.

The heart of the wise is in the house of mourning; but the heart of fools is in the house of mirth (Ecclesiastes 7: 3–4; King James Version).

This warning against laughter is a warning against succumbing to pleasure in the world; the implication is that laughter only offers short–lived fulfilment, and in the long–run a pious, serious, sorrowful life is better for the soul. Sorrow might be painful, but pain is ennobling.

In the first years of Christianity, Christians sought to define themselves against behaviour associated with pagan Rome, and this was one factor in shaping their attitude to laughter. For the early Christians there was virtue in self–restraint because it contrasted with the debauchery and excesses of Rome. Laughter came to be allied with such excesses and, given its physical dimension, with the body and possible lack of control over base instincts. Later in middle ages this mistrust of laughter continued: many Christian writers banned laughter altogether as they associated it with a variety of sins; Barry Sanders, for instance, notes that for Hildegard of Bingen laughter was linked to sin because it offered a relief from labour—in other words it offered relief from a punishment meted out by God for defying him in the Garden of Eden. We only need laughter because we are sinful, and we should aspire instead to be in Heaven where, purged of our sins, we may experience laughter–free bliss (*Sudden Glory*, 129).

The Church emphasised piety and seriousness, then, deeming laughter to be something irreverent that mocked Heaven; indeed it was considered one of the worst vices for Christian monks, as Jerry Palmer has written:

In the earliest monastic regulations (in the fifth century) laughter is condemned as the grossest breach of the rule of silence, and later it is considered as a breach of the rule of humility; it is also considered the greatest dirtying of the mouth, which should act as a filter for good and evil to enter and leave the body; therefore it must be prevented. (*Taking Humour Seriously*, 44)

Though the Church authorities tried various methods to outlaw laughter, there is evidence that this didn't work and that jokes flourished even in monasteries. Eventually the hard line on laughter eased somewhat and in medieval times the Church attempted to make a distinction between good and bad laughter. The smile came to be seen as an acceptable alternative to laughter, and was eventually deemed to be something that should be cultivated as evidence of good humour, sound character, and even saintliness.

It has often been noted that Jesus never laughs in the Bible, although he is shown weeping more than once. The issue of Jesus's apparent lack of humour has been a huge one for many Christian theologians. If laughter is an essential human quality, something that sets us apart from animals, then signs of humour and laughter become an important factor in showing Christ's human status. Medieval theologians scrutinised the Bible assiduously for evidence of humour, and there was even an annual conference on this issue organised by the University of Paris in the thirteenth century. Genuine evidence of Christ's humour is very hard to find, although Simon Critchley makes reference to the story of the marriage at Cana (John 2: 1–11) as a possible contender. This is the occasion of Christ's first miracle, and the story suggests that Mary ordered Jesus to help out when the host informed her that the wine had run dry: 'They have no more wine' she tells Jesus, to which he replies, 'Woman, my time has not yet come.' Mary then seems to take the matter out of his hands by telling the servants to, 'Do whatever he tells you;' at this point Jesus gives in and performs the miracle. Critchley compares this scene to Monty Python's *The Life of Brian*, and Brian's mother's excellent line: 'he's not the Messiah, he's a very naughty boy.' I'm not sure the comparison is that convincing, although there is perhaps a parallel in the potentially humorous dynamic between a Messiah and his mother. The fact that Jesus is willing to submit and do his mother's bidding despite his elevated status perhaps signals a capacity for humour. As will be seen, however, humour and laughter have featured in the history of Christianity in more radical ways.

8.2 Holy Fools

In the discussion of carnival humour earlier I mentioned the Feast of Fools, and this is something that began in the Church. It was an annual ecclesiastical festival in which priests and clerks would engage in impious activities, parodying Church dignitaries and rituals. In terms of Christian theology, the laughter associated with the Feast of Fools symbolised vice and human failings: the low behaviour at the Feast represented the lowly nature of man and his urgent need for spiritual deliverance; in practise, however, it probably served a similar function to a lay carnival, offering the clergy a chance to let off steam, a welcome, and one would imagine psychologically necessary diversion.

Humour and laughter have been seen as a route to the spiritual life by some Christians: there are certainly comic elements associated with the phenomenon of the Holy Fool. The sixth century Christian monk, Simeon is the patron saint of Holy Fools; he adopted this role in his efforts to serve the Lord, and his behaviour often had a comic facet, characterized as it was by clowning, bizarre pranks and feigned madness. So–called Foolishness–for–Christ has a long tradition in both Western and Eastern Christianity, and variations of the Holy Fool phenomenon can be seen in other religions too, including Judaism and Islam. The purpose is often to use clowning, grotesquery, and extreme behaviour as a way of shocking people out of conventional ways of thinking in order to make them more receptive to the otherness of religious experience. There are references to holy folly in the Bible itself: Peter L. Berger mentions David's insane naked dancing in front of the Ark of the Covenant in the Second Book of Samuel as a clear example. He sees significance also in Jesus's statement that we should try to be more like children, and in his decision to enter Jerusalem on a donkey (with its traditional associations with folly). Berger makes the point too that, in the final moments of his life, 'Jesus was crowned as the king of folly' by the Roman soldiers who made him endure a mock coronation with his crown of thorns and reed sceptre. In other words the notion of folly seems to have a place in the Christian narrative; for Berger the behaviour of the fool becomes a way of deprivileging reason, offering a fresh perspective on the apparent irrationality of faith: when we encounter holy folly, 'the empirical world, far from being paramount, is disclosed as being very finite indeed. The madness of the fool is now seen to be the infinitely more profound truth.'[49] Folly can offer insight into the fleeting nature of the empirical world by allowing us accesses to another, non–rational way of thinking. For people without faith, faith belongs to the realm of fantasy; however the fool's madness turns the reality/fantasy hierarchy on its head: for the fool the *real* fantasy is mundane reality. The fool refuses to partake of reality, with its faith–denying rationality. Instead he embraces the ostensibly irrational, which refuses to be constrained by logic and reason; in this way folly becomes wisdom, as Enid Welsford writes in her history of the fool:

> The theist believes in possible beatitude, because he disbe-lieves in the dignified isolation of humanity. To him, there-fore […] comedy is serious […] because it is a foretaste of the truth; the Fool is wiser than the Humanist, and clownage is less frivolous than the deification of humanity.[50]

Comedy offers a preview of whatever lies beyond the human; it reveals the latter's misplaced preoccupation with its own affairs, and its intolerance of anything that contravenes the codes of reason. In this sense humour loses its connotations of frivolousness, and can even provide a 'way in' to religious conceptions of truth and wisdom.

So this reveals a way in which humour can be compatible with religion, and even facilitate religious insight. Indeed, the idea of the Holy Fool continues to inspire some Christians: there is a UK based performance troupe called Holy Fools UK who perform as clowns at churches. The membership is drawn from all denominations and their mission is to use clowning as a way of promoting their faith.

---

49 Peter L. Berger. *Redeeming Laughter: The Comic Dimension of Human Experience* (Berlin: Walter de Gruyter & Co, 1997) 195.
50 Enid Welsford, *The Fool: His Social and Literary History* (New York: Anchor Books, 1961) 326–7.

Creative Writing Exercise

> Create a character who feels that everyone in the world apart from them is living in a fiction produced by an evil genius. The fiction depends on logic and reason for its existence, but every time someone has an illogical or irrational thought, a crack appears in the fiction. Laughter at bizarre humour is its biggest enemy. If enough people can be made to entertain or be entertained by so-called 'irrational thoughts' then the fiction will collapse altogether and a higher truth will be revealed. It is your character's mission to try to achieve this.

8.3 Judaism and Humour

Arguably the association between Judaism and humour is stronger than in Christianity; certainly there is a tradition of humour in Jewish culture that can be traced back centuries and is still with us in the modern world. Once again it is worth considering Ted Cohen's thoughts on this issue. According to Cohen, Jewish humour is particularly associated with jokes that deal in incomprehensibility, and humour that offers bizarre, apparently illogical logic. He quotes the following joke as an example:

> A man is lying asleep in bed with his wife one night when she wakes him, saying, 'close the window; it's cold outside.'
> He grunts, rolls over, and goes back to sleep.
> His wife nudges him. 'Close the window; it's cold outside.'
> He moans, pulls the blankets closer, and goes back to sleep.
> Now his wife kicks him firmly and pushes him with both hands. 'Go on. Close the window; it's cold outside.'
> Grumbling, he slides out of bed, shuffles to the window, and bangs it closed. Glaring at his wife he says, 'So now it's warm outside?'. (Ted Cohen, *Jokes*, 46)

This joke makes no sense on one level, and yet there does seem to be a weird logic to the punch line. The narrative is structured around a conflict that ends with a statement that doesn't resolve it; rather it adds another dimension to it, which seems to justify the husband's initial reluctance to yield to his wife's request. It suggests the futility of his action. While he has agreed to his wife's demand he also implies that he has wasted his time in doing so. We get the impression that the characters in this narrative could continue to argue in perpetuity: the widow is closed but the issue is not. Cohen finds philosophical precedent for such jokes in the Hebrew Bible and the Talmud, and suggests that they suit Judaism because argument is so fundamental to the Jewish tradition; there is no final word or answer in Judaism: when someone studies the Jewish faith their engagement is characterised by never–ending debate and argument; there is, to use Cohen's words, 'no systematic finality. In a word there is no Pope' (Cohen, *Jokes*, 66). The Jewish tradition more readily accepts the incomprehensible then; it accepts that life is baffling and that there are no simple answers—just like there is no end to the conflict between the chilly woman and her weary husband. There are certainly many Jewish jokes not cited by Cohen that would appear to support his argument, not least this one: 'What do you get when you lock two Jews in a room? Three opinions.' Here is another:

> A rabbi was in hospital recovering from a heart attack when a representative of the congregation visited him.
> 'Rabbi, he said, 'I have good news and bad news.'
> 'First tell me the good news'
> 'On behalf of the board I am here to wish you a speedy recovery.'
> 'That's great" said the rabbi, 'what's the bad news?'
> 'The vote was 7 to 4.'

Again this is clearly a joke which has the topic of argument at its heart, and which implies that at least one dispute remains unresolved!

According to Cohen there is evidence of God laughing in the Talmud; he cites a reference to Elijah who claims to have seen it: God apparently laughs when he hears about human attempts to interpret one of his laws so that they might better understand his will; however, the humans in question end up ignoring God's own opinion on the matter, constructing instead an interpretation of God's will at odds with God's own statement. This is a laugh at the expense of the human condition, then, and an indication that there is something about our predicament that we should find funny: principally its absurdity. It also suggests that when confronted by absurdity laughter is a valid response; perhaps the only response.

Cohen also offers an interesting interpretation of the story of Abraham in Genesis. When God tells the 100 year old Abraham that he is going to have a son, Abraham laughs, as does his 90 year old wife Sarah. This is understandable, of course. However Sarah is frightened of offending God, and when he makes reference to her laughter she denies it. Importantly, God insists on her acknowledging it. It could be argued that Sarah's laughter at God's plan is indicative of her lack of faith, but Cohen has another reading: he points to the passage following the birth of her son, Isaac, where she says: 'God has brought me laughter; everyone who hears will laugh with me.' (Genesis 21: 1–7). For Cohen this could refer both to the gift of Isaac, whose name means laughter, and to Sarah's laughter when she heard God's intention. Laughter is God's gift, then, and this notion is further supported by God's decision to have Abraham spare Isaac from sacrifice, instructing him to kill a ram instead; in effect God is instructing Abraham to set laughter free: 'directing that laughter be freed, let loose in the world.' (Cohen, *Jokes*, 55). As suggested, the laughter signifies helplessness in the face of ignorance; it acknowledges our limitations, and perhaps provides the only consolation. Cohen states his thesis in the following terms:

> What I claim is that Abraham, Sarah, and those of us who laugh at these jokes are all laughing at the same kind of thing. It is something not fully comprehensible, and our laughter is an acceptance of the thing in its incomprehensibility. It is the acceptance of the world, a world that is endlessly incomprehensible, always baffling, a world that is beyond us and yet our world. (Cohen, *Jokes*, 60)

Given their history of debating apparently irresolvable arguments, Jewish people are inclined toward this kind of laughter, according to Cohen; they are more willing than most to accept the incomprehensible 'in their wonder,' and thus for them laughter becomes 'an echo of faith' that somewhere, beyond the ostensibly illogical, lies meaning.

It has to be said that, while there are jokes that support Cohen's view, it is possible to find examples of Jewish joking that seem to close arguments down rather than leave them unresolved; also there are examples that appear to abandon the quest for meaning altogether: for instance there is a well-known humorous Yiddish proverb that goes, 'If you want to alleviate your worries, wear tighter shoes,' which would work as an effective way of terminating most arguments! Still, Cohen's thesis is an interesting attempt to establish a parallel between jokes and the narrative that purports to give meaning to the Jewish experience.

Creative Writing Exercise

> Try to create a comic argument between two stubborn characters that involves an apparently irresolvable issue. For instance, 'it is more acceptable to shoot birds than rabbits because rabbits don't shit on your head.' Have them discuss the issue from as many angles as possible for as long as possible until the futility of the argument becomes comically apparent. This is one particularly entertaining way of exploring the comic possibilities of illogical-logic, incomprehensibility, and the farcicality of the human situation.

8.4 Humour and Buddhism

Humour has a role in Buddhism, perhaps more so than with any other religion, but this was not always the case. In the early stages of its development in ancient India, humour and laughter were actively discouraged by Buddhist masters; it was actually an offence for monks to laugh in public. Michel Clasquin offers the following quote from Buddhist scripture as an example of early Buddhist attitudes to humour:

> One should not go amidst the houses with loud laughter. Whoever out of disrespect, laughing a great laugh, goes amidst the houses, there is an offence of wrongdoing (but) there is no offence if it is unintentional, if he is not thinking, if he does not know, if he is ill, if he only smiles when the matter is one for laughing, if there are accidents, if he is mad, if he is the

first wrong–doer.[51]

It was felt that laughter should be kept in check then; however this can be contrasted with the approach to humour and laughter found in Zen Buddhism, which emerged in China around fifteen hundred years later. Here there this a much more positive view, and the difference can be seen in Buddhist iconography: the serene, but essentially humourless image of the Indian Buddha is replaced by the corpulent Chinese laughing Buddha. Also humour comes to occupy a central role in the education of monks in the ways of Zen:

> humour in Zen Buddhism has been changed from something to be avoided if at all possible to a teaching device in its own right. Time and again we read of Zen monks and their masters laughing uproariously, of revered teachers clowning around, playing the fool, joking even about things ordinarily held sacred by other Buddhists, not excluding the Buddha himself. (Michel Clasquin, 'Real Buddhas Don't Laugh,' 99)

For Clasquin, the differences in attitude reflect different philosophical positions on humour and laughter. The Buddhists of ancient India tended to think of humour in terms of superiority. In the extract cited from ancient Indian scripture, for instance, the underlying assumption is that laughter is inappropriate because the monks would be using it to elevate their own position in relation to the people of 'the houses,' and hence disrespecting them. Even if their position is indeed superior, this superiority should be shown through humility, not through boastful laughter. Clasquin draws an interesting parallel between this and how people from higher social strata in general relate to humour: 'If laughter expresses a feeling of superiority, and if one is already convinced of one's superior status, then laughter becomes otiose and humour, the object of laughter, an unnecessary luxury' ('Real Buddhas Don't Laugh,' 111). This conception of humour can be contrasted with that among Chinese Zen Buddhists. They think of humour more in terms of incongruity,

---

51 Michel Clasquin, 'Real Buddhas Don't Laugh: Attitudes towards Humour and Laughter in Ancient India and China,' *Social Identities*, Volume 7, Number 1, 2001, 97–116 (97).

and this is why it is valued as a useful teaching aid. Zen Buddhists feel that before we can achieve enlightenment we must jettison our attachment to everything that shapes our thinking. We need to relinquish conventional models of thought, and we can only do so if we find ways of circumventing the rational mind. The task is to free ourselves from the ego and the notion that it has any meaning in the broader scheme. The incongruous nature of humour can help us to do this; humour can invert concepts and create startling contrasts in ways that shock students out of their predictable thought patterns, enabling them to side–step rational thought, opening the mind to 'truths' that would ordinarily seem counterintuitive. This is the function of kōans—the questions or statements given by Zen masters to their students to help them in their quest for enlightenment. The answers to these questions cannot be deduced by logic, or with reference to existing knowledge, but must be arrived at via intuition. In Western thinking the kōan has come to denote an ambiguous or unanswerable question, but Zen teaching does anticipate an answer, although there may be more than one. The student is asked to reflect on the kōan until they arrive at a satisfactory response. Kōans are often given by the master at the conclusion of a dialogue, then the student is given time to consider the potential meaning. Perhaps the most famous example of a kōan, for instance, is: 'what is the sound of one hand clapping?' This question itself defies logic and as such invites an illogical or humorous response. Occasionally the kōan is intended to help the student understand the irrelevance of hierarchy, reinforcing the notion that nothing is better than anything else; or they can be employed to reveal how outwardly dissimilar things are actually united in essence, helping students to think in terms of unity rather than duality. The following well–known kōan, 'Echo Asks about Buddha,' potentially serves both functions:

> A monk asked Hogen, 'I, Echo, ask you, Master. What is Buddha?'
>
> Hogen said, 'You are Echo.'

You can see how this might encourage a student to comprehend the irrelevance of the distinction between himself and Buddha, and of the hierarchy between master and pupil. It has the characteristics of humour, of course, because there is an incongruity between what Echo expects to hear and what the master actually says: as with a joke, the student must move beyond conventional thinking in order to get the point.

Creative Writing Exercise

Try to construct a question/answer style kōan that expresses the illusory nature of difference in the way that the 'Echo Asks about Buddha' kōan does. Experiment with different questions and off-beat answers until you have one that you feel might conceivably be germane to the issue. Think of it in terms of writing a joke that only another joker on the same wavelength will understand!

9. Postmodernism and Humour

Pause and Reflect

Consider the potential relationship between humour and uncertainty. What are the implications of not taking *anything* seriously?

Humour is very often a feature of the various cultural phenomena that are referred to as postmodern, such as the kitsch sculptures of Jeff Koons, the films of Quentin Tarrantino, the novels of Thomas Pynchon, and so on. Cultural products of this kind began to emerge in the late twentieth century and commonly feature playfulness, self–consciousness, irony, and a reluctance to take anything—even them-selves—seriously. Other characteristics include a refusal to be cat-egorised as either high art or low art, and a tendency to mix cultural codes from both. Postmodern art products often undermine their own status as original works by endlessly referencing their dependence on pre–exiting texts; they also tend to refute the possibility of transcend-ent, eternal value or truth. In other words they reflect what might be called a postmodern view of the world, characterised in general terms by mistrust of certainty.

The so–called postmodern condition has been interpreted in a variety of ways. Theorists like Jean Baudrillard (1929–2007) and Fredric Jameson (1934–), for instance, link it to shifts in the social structure, and developments in technology that have created an image–dominated world which undermines our engagement with reality. Jean Francois Lyotard (1924–1998) relates postmodernism to our scepticism toward so–called master–narratives: narratives that purport to explain the world in an all–encompassing way. John Barth (1930–) and Umberto Eco (1932–) see postmodernism partly as a symptom of cultural exhaustion, and the impossibility of being original in contemporary life. Barth and Eco's view is that we are mired in the 'already said,' and cannot escape from cliché, except through irony and humour. In addition, postmodernism is often seen as complementing the ideas of poststructuralist philosophers like Jacques Derrida (1930–2004), whose work addresses the arbitrary/unstable nature of meaning in language, and of psychoanalysts like Jacques Lacan (1901–1981) who suggest that the idea of a coherent self is an illusion. According to Lance Olsen, humour pairs well with postmodern thinking because:

> both the comic and the postmodern attempt to subvert all centres of authority—including their own—and because they both ultimately deride univocal visions, toppling bigots, cranks, and pompous idiots as they go [...] Both seek through radical incongruity of form to short circuit the dominant culture's repressive impulses.[52]

So for Olsen it is partly the subversive potential of humour that appeals to the postmodern sensibility. This debunking facet of postmodernism has been criticised by many theorists, including Terry Eagleton (1943–) and Christopher Norris (1947–) who see postmodernism as an intellectual dead–end. They feel that a position that critiques all positions can never be constructive. In its insistence on resisting master–narratives, postmodernism is at odds with Enlightenment notions of reason and progress: for postmodernists this is just another reductive narrative that excludes alternative points of view (for instance, whose idea of progress are we talking about?) Postmodernism has also been associated with relativism: this is the idea that there are no truths, and that all questions of value are dependent on context and perspective. However, Olsen sees the relationship between postmodernism and humour in largely positive terms: while postmodernism and humour can indeed be destructive, debunking and negative, they can also be constructive:

> Both focus on process rather than conclusion. Both embrace plurality, an abundance of language games, and the idea that

52 Lance Olsen, *Circus of the Mind in Motion: Postmodernism and the Comic Vision* (Detroit, MI: Wayne State UP, 1990) 31.

the universe is a text that may be written in host of equally acceptable ways. And both therefore understand [...] that 'pure play is one of the main bases of civilisation'. (Lance Olsen, *Circus*, 32)

For Olsen, there is optimism and value in the notion of humorous play itself: while it always resists conclusions and certainties, it is also continually creative, inventing new ways of seeing and thinking. Humour and play always keep potentially oppressive and limiting authorities in check, but importantly for thinkers like Olson, they can do so without destroying them. There is a sense in which a postmodern concept is one that returns after it has been stripped of its fundamentalist ambitions; that is, it returns once comedy has deconstructed it and taught us not to take it too seriously. In order to illustrate this consider how Umberto Eco describes the 'postmodern attitude;' it is that:

of a man who loves a very cultivated woman and knows he cannot say to her 'I love you madly,' because he knows that she knows (and that she knows that he knows) that these words have already been written by Barbara Cartland. Still there is a solution. He can say, 'As Barbara Cartland would put it, I love you madly.' At this point, having avoided false innocence, having said clearly that it is no longer possible to speak innocently, he will nevertheless have said what he wanted to say to the woman: that he loves her, but he loves her in an age of lost innocence.[53]

Here irony is used to acknowledge this statement's status as a cliché, but the irony doesn't destroy the statement: the man still manages says what he feels, it's just that his words have been stripped of any claim to originality. The fact that humour and irony can do this kind of thing is valuable for postmodernists: because it can make assertions and simultaneously undermine them, humorous narrative can avoid becoming authoritarian and absolutist. There is no context in which subjective individuals can agree on final answers to funda-

---

53 Umberto Eco, quoted in Brian McHale, *Constructing Postmodernism* (London: Routledge, 1992), 145.

mental questions, but thanks to humour and irony postmodern narratives can create an arena in which it is possible to present a debate in a qualified way, with an implicit reservation that uncertainty must be acknowledged. Humorous narratives work like fictions in this sense—they can create a field for debate where doubt is always recognised, and argument proceeds from a position that accepts subjectivity. Indeed, for many thinkers, fiction, particularly the comic novel, can play an important role in philosophy, and it is worth saying a little about this before we proceed. Consider these words from the American philosopher, Richard Rorty (1931–2007), discussing the distinction between traditional philosophers and novelists:

> The philosopher's essentialist approach [...] is a disingenuous way of saying: what matters for me takes precedence over what matters for you, entitles me to ignore what happens to you, because I am in touch with something—reality—which you are not. The novelist's rejoinder to this: it is comical to believe that one human being is more in touch with something nonhuman than another human being. It is comical to use one's quest for the ineffable Other as an excuse for ignoring other people's quite different quests. It is comical to think that there is something called Truth.[54]

Rorty was a philosopher who recognised fiction's potential as a space for philosophical inquiry and argument, and this sense of the value of fiction became increasingly apparent to many thinkers in the late twentieth century. Novels can demonstrate what Milan Kundera calls, 'the wisdom of uncertainty' (*The Art of the Novel*, 7), and as such offer the possibility of the kind of qualified debate that postmodernism insists on; indeed, as will be seen, it was the ambition of many so–called postmodern novels to use comedy and irony to ensure that the 'wisdom of uncertainty' plays a key role in how philosophical issues are addressed.

---

54 Richard Rorty, quoted in Christopher Norris, *The Truth About Postmodernism* (London: Blackwell, 1993) 282.

Creative Writing Exercise

Write the tale of the Christian Nativity as a short story, keeping the tone sombre and respectful. Describe the interior of the stable, the dialogue between those present, etc. Now rewrite it and attempt to weave some humour into the narrative; perhaps try exaggerating here and there in order to emphasise the odd circumstances of the occasion, and the idea of a virgin birth. What effect does the humour have on how a reader might relate to the story?

9.1 John A. McClure: The Comically Cosmic

The American literary critic John A. McClure has argued that postmodern comic fiction finds ways of exploring religious issues, and reclaiming religious ideas that have been progressively marginalised in the West through years of increasing secularization. In his view most postmodern philosophers—he cites Jameson and Lyotard specifically—have assumed that postmodernism is part of a history of secularization and that the spiritual lacks contemporary relevance. For McClure, however, spiritual enquiry continues in the comically inflected novels of postmodern writers like Thomas Pynchon, among others. Such novels are able to challenge the authority of reason, but at the same time create a space for religious thinking; in Pynchon's comic novels, for instance, 'long discredited ways of seeing and saying both Western and non–Western stage a complex kind of come–back.'[55] For McClure it is the humorous facet of the work that facilitates this come–back:

> Wild and defiantly unrealistic exercises in irreverent citation, genre–splicing, excess, caricature, and the grotesque, they so run against the grain of realistic [...] seriousness that it seems absurd, at first, to treat them as taking any issues seriously. And yet if they seem comically irreverent, they are also comically cosmic: they address sacred alternatives to secular constructions of reality in ways that invest these alternatives with a certain authority and invite us to reflection If we accept this invitation, of course, the joke may be on us: there's always

55 John A. McClure. 'Postmodern/Post–Secular: Contemporary Fiction and Spirituality,' *Modern Fiction Studies*, 41, 1, Spring, 1995, 141–163 (146).

the suggestion, in these texts, that any kind of faith, secular
or spiritual, is folly. But if we refuse the invitation, the case is
the same: for the texts also suggest that secularism is a form
of mystification and that those who accept its definition of
possibility are victims of a world historical ruse (McClure,
'Postmodern/Post–Secular,' 149).

Such texts position spiritual narratives alongside secular narratives
on equal terms, simultaneously satirising and asserting both, using
humour to 'mock advocacy and practice it' and offering a 'combination of cosmic irreverence and comic advocacy' (McClure,
'Postmodern/Post–Secular,' 148). McClure cites Thomas Pynchon's
Gravity's Rainbow (1973) as a book which introduces a range of
different spiritual narratives alongside conventional rationalism
in a story more critical of the latter than the former. Similarly, he
argues that Pynchon's *Vineland* (1990) playfully juxtaposes secular and non–secular ontologies (planes or constructions of reality) in
a way that 'recapitulates and implicitly reinstates earlier modelling
of a sacred or at least enchanted universe' (McClure, 'Postmodern/
Post–Secular,' 150). The distinction between secular and non–secular
ontological realms is often blurred in such texts, and as such, according to McClure, they have an 'unworlding' effect on the reader, rendering it difficult or meaningless to distinguish between the so–called
supernatural or the mundane. The non–secular narratives in question
often have affinities with those explored by experimental theologians
such as Carol Christ, Charlene Spretnak, and Margot Alder. These
thinkers are outside the realm of mainstream philosophy and theology, and show an interest in, among other things, immanence and the
idea of the spiritual as something integral to the world, rather than
as something that presides over the world; their thinking also often
incorporates an interest in spiritual interconnectedness of a kind
associated with pantheism, and other non–traditional conceptions of
the universe. In its 'ontological playfulness' the work of postmodern
novelists like Pynchon offers a 'reaffirmation of premodern ontologies' (McClure, 'Postmodern/Post–Secular,' 150), using humour to
explore and reclaim philosophies previously marginalised by post–
Enlightenment rationalism. In this sense, then, humour becomes a

method of facilitating radical theological and philosophical debate.

9.2 Humour as Philosophy

The phenomenon of humour actually becoming philosophy—that is creating a space for philosophical inquiry—is one that has interesting associations with postmodernism. Obviously humorous texts have always done this—from Aristophanes to Samuel Beckett—but this has tended to be restricted to the realm of high art. One of the functions of humour in postmodern texts has been to close the gap between high art and popular culture: humour is entertaining after all, and as Cicero noted it has the capacity to augment the charm of any narrative. Moreover, humour's reluctance to take itself seriously can create a 'wisdom of uncertainty' appealing to those suspicious of absolutist assertions. In recent years several books have appeared which examine how examples of popular culture can work as a vehicle for philosophical exploration and discussion; many focus on what might be called postmodern comedy. For example books such as *Seinfeld and Philosophy: A Book About Everything and Nothing* (1999) and *The Simpsons and Philosophy: The D' oh! Of Homer* (2001), collect essays on these shows written by philosophers. They consider the philosophical issues raised by the shows, and how they bring them to a popular audience. So, for instance, *The Simpsons and Philosophy* contains an essay on the representation of hypocrisy in Springfield which is seen to raise questions about the ethics of hypocrisy, and whether hypocrisy is always immoral. Another discusses a classic *Simpsons* episode, 'They Saved Lisa's Brain,' which explores the viability of Springfield as a political utopia: a version of Plato's *Republic*. This is worth discussing in a little more detail. Inspired by Lisa, the Springfield branch of Mensa (comprised of Dr Hibbert, Comic Book Guy, Principal Skinner, and Professor Frink) form a 'council of learned citizens' who manage to take over the town. In an attempt to create what Principal Skinner calls 'a new Athens' they begin taking measures to ban violent sport, make adjustments to traffic flow, and so on. However, as Paul A. Cantor points out:

> in a variant of the dialectic of enlightenment, the abstract

rationality and benevolent universalism of the intellectual junta soon prove to be a fraud. The Mensa members begin to disagree among themselves and it becomes evident that their claim to represent the public interest masks a number of private agendas.[56]

The physicist Stephen Hawking arrives in Springfield as a representative of brainy people, and upbraids the so–called learned citizens for their failure. Homer leads an insurgent force of stupid people against the Mensa elite, and 'the attempt to bring about a rule of philosopher–kings in Springfield ends ignominiously' (Paul A. Cantor, 'The Simpsons,' 177). The episode closes with Homer and Hawking sharing a beer, and Homer about to explain to him his theory of a doughnut shaped universe. The show makes an important intellectual point about the difficulty of imposing theory on reality, and offers a defence of the ordinary man against intellectualism, 'in a way both the common man and the intellectual can understand and enjoy' (Paul A. Cantor, 'The Simpsons,' 178). Again this is an example of humour, this time in the shape of popular comedy, operating as philosophy.

Pause and Reflect

Can you think of any similarities between stand–up comedy and philosophy?

The phenomenon of humour becoming a vehicle for philosophical ideas can be seen in the realm stand–up comedy too. A number of philosophers have drawn parallels between the strategies employed by stand–up comedians and philosophers. John Morreall, for instance, points out that stand–ups and philosophers often explore issues in the form of dialogue, creating imaginary characters to represent conflicting points of view; both spend time questioning their experience, taking puzzling everyday events and subjecting them to analysis. This activity involves an element of detachment and impartial reflection

56 Paul A. Cantor, 'The Simpsons: Atomistic Politics and the Nuclear Family,' in William Irwin, Mark T. Conard, Aeon J. Skoble, eds., *The Simpsons and Philosophy: The D' oh! Of Homer* (Illinois: Carus Publishing Company, 2001) 160–178 (177).

that is common to both too. Also stand–up comedians and philosophers enjoy shifts in perspective, and the activity of seeing familiar
things in fresh ways; both utilize thought experiments and scenarios
prefaced with the phrase, 'What if…' Stand–ups and philosophers
also share a similar approach to authority and accepted wisdom, and
are more likely to critically challenge tradition.

The kind of stand–up comedian that Morreall has in mind emerged
relatively recently in our culture: he is referring to the kind of stand–
up who does not tell prefabricated jokes, but whose act is structured
around observation. With one or two exceptions (notably perhaps the
American humorist Will Hay), this kind of observational comedian
didn't really begin to appear until the second half of the twentieth
century. Increasingly in America, for instance, observational
comedians like Lenny Bruce and Mort Sahl began to eclipse one–
liner style comedians such as Henny Youngman and Milton Berle.
In British culture this shift came a little later, and is associated with
the alternative comedy revolution of the nineteen eighties. In other
words, the move away from closed jokes to open observational comic
narrative parallels the emergence of postmodernism, which is seen as
a late twentieth century phenomenon. It is another example of the
gap between high and low culture closing, and of philosophy being
relocated in the arena of popular comedy. Lenny Bruce (1925–1966)
was perhaps the first high profile comedian to be discussed in these
terms: the title of Frank Kofsky's book, *Lenny Bruce: The Comedian
as Social Critic and Secular Moralist* (1974) tells us something
about how Bruce has been interpreted. Bruce stand–up routines
such as 'Christ and Moses' are 'What if…' scenarios with a clear
philosophical thesis. In the latter Moses visits modern America to
witness how contemporary advocates of religion are infatuated with
money; Bruce's premise is stated quite clearly: 'any man who calls
himself a religious leader and owns more than one suit is a hustler as
long as there is someone in the world who has no suit at all.'[57] Mostly
Bruce addressed philosophical issues from the point of view of a
sceptic, but there are also examples of comedians offering the kind

---

57 Lenny Bruce, quoted in Frank Kofsky, *Lenny Bruce: The Comedian as Social
Critic and Secular Moralist* (New York: Monad Press, 1974) 49.

of 'comically cosmic' religious assertions that McCulre observes in postmodern novels. For instance, the late American comedian Bill Hicks (1961–1994) disparages traditional religious institutions as vehemently as Lenny Bruce did, but at the same he creates comic routines that seem to reclaim non–traditional religious ideas. As Paul Outhwaite says in his study of Hicks:

> He believed 'our bodies are an illusion,' and that the mind was humanity's most powerful component, that its openness is what guides experience after death. It is why, in Hicks' comedy, God, the mind, spirituality and the soul are inextricably linked.[58]

Similar attitudes can be seen in the work of the contemporary British stand–up comedian Russell Brand. Like Hicks he often seems to simultaneously disparage and celebrate religious ideas, offering what McClure would call a combination of mockery and advocacy. An example can be seen in an interview where he discusses his performance preparations, which involve locking himself in a toilet cubicle to carry out a breathing ritual that, he claims, augments his sense of spiritual connection:

> Striving for cleanliness, I find myself…inhaling deeper than one would like, to try to breathe myself into some clear–headed Zen like state so that I'm focussed […] The ritualization of it […] is to move from a state of the individual into a consciousness of connection of being at one with higher things.[59]

Brand strives for an experience of cosmic unity, but the fact that he seeks it in a toilet cubicle is comically at odds with the elevated objective: it is an example of advocacy (of Buddhist practices in this case) being qualified by mockery, simultaneously installing and subverting a sense of the spiritual. He takes this qualified sense of the spiritual with him on stage and it becomes a foundation for his act. Often he interrogates it and explores its implications, either via 'What if…'

---

58 Paul Outhwaite, *One Consciousness: An Analysis of Bill Hicks' Comedy* (Middlesbrough: D.M. Productions, 2003) 202.
59 Russell Brand. *Skinned: In Interview With Frank Skinner.* (Channel 4 documentary broadcast, November, 2009).

scenarios, or by reflecting on his life experiences. In one routine, for instance, he discusses being on a film set where he was given a caravan, unlike the bigger stars who had trailers. In an effort to appease his jealousy he says to himself:

> You are a spiritual being, detach yourself: it doesn't matter, it's irrelevant. Your soul is eternal, the material world is transient – do not become attached to the caravan: worrying about the caravan is ultimately irrelevant. And then I'd see them going into their lovely trailer and think: You fucking cunts.[60]

Brand juxtaposes the ideal of spiritual striving with the reality of failure. The incongruity is exploited for comic effect, and the punch line comically qualifies his alleged piety, constructing Brand and his inability to achieve spiritual detachment as the butt of the joke. The humour introduces a degree of ambiguity, of course, and we are forced to ask whether the punch line negates the ideals expressed, or whether the central message of spiritual permanence is retained. Might it even be argued that the humour gives the spiritual sentiments a viability they would not otherwise possess? Certainly the humour serves to preclude the possibility of cliché: Brand's spiritual words would sound corny outside the comic context (without the punch line). His readiness admit his fallibility meanwhile reflects a culture suspicious of certainty, offsetting the kind of absolutism associated with religious dogma: might this go some way toward reclaiming it? In other words, in keeping with postmodernism, Brand articulates religious ideas that, potentially at least, return after being stripped of their dogmatic and absolutist associations. This seems like an example of 'cosmic irreverence and comic advocacy;' and the possibility of advocacy depends partly on the presence of the comedy. Whether this ironic recycling of religious ideas qualifies Hicks and Brand as postmodern theologians or philosophers is obviously questionable, but, as with Bruce, they are often discussed in these terms by fans and critics, and at the very least they offer an alternative arena in which philosophical issues can be probed.

In the late twentieth century there was an increasing willingness

---

60 Russell Brand, *Doing Life Live* (Universal Pictures, 2007) DVD.

among scholars to treat comedy—particularly stand–up—as a legitimate site of enquiry and debate on a whole host of issues. Indeed, stand–up comedy has almost been assigned a privileged status in modern culture; studies have appeared with titles such as 'Stand–up Comedy as Rhetorical Argument,' 'Stand–up Comedian as Anthropologist,' 'Stand–up Comedy as Social and Cultural Mediation,' among many others.[61] In the latter, for instance, Lawrence Minz, maintains that stand–up comedians have a 'license for deviate behaviour and expression' that gives them freedom to express 'truths' that cannot normally be voiced in society; as a result they can interrogate and materially affect their social world; they can 'explore, affirm, deny, and ultimately [...] change its structure and values.'[62] As seen earlier, to some extent Cicero was the first philosopher to see humour's potential to do this kind of thing. As Barry Sanders notes, 'For Cicero, the orator closely resembles the stand–up comic, dazzling the audience with wit and imagination, shaped into little "shticks," and causing every member of the audience to wonder what is true and what is not' (Barry Sanders, *Sudden Glory,* 122). The fact that the audience cannot decide what is fact or fiction in comedy is part of its power; it is what gives comedians the 'licence for deviate behaviour' that Laurence Minz identifies: comedians, even as they express so–called 'truths,' are always able to say, 'only joking'. Thus humour can make philosophical issues palatable in several ways: it can make them entertaining, and therefore accessible to a larger audience; it can reinvigorate them by detaching them from cliché, and it can create a space in which no single idea is privileged over another.

Creative Writing Exercise

Write a stand–up monologue around one or both of the following 'What if...' scenarios:

61 See Andrea Greenbaum, 'Stand–up Comedy as Rhetorical Argument: An Investigation of Comic Culture,' *Humor*, 12, 1, 1999, 33–46; and Stephanie Koziski, 'Stand–up Comedian as Anthropologist: Intentional Culture Critic,' *Journal of Popular Culture*, 18, 2, 1984, 57–76.
62 Lawrence Mintz, 'Stand–up Comedy as Social and Cultural Mediation,' *American Quarterly* 37, 1985, 71–80 (73–74).

What if the Devil found himself auditioning for the *X Factor*?
What if Gandhi was reincarnated to find himself in a Twitter exchange with Lady Ga Ga?

9.3 Susan Purdie: Joking and the Unstable Self

In her book, *Comedy: The Mastery of Discourse* (1993) Susan Purdie offers a postmodern theory of humour that reworks Freud's view of tendentious jokes in an interesting way. We saw above how Freud felt that jokers may reference taboos in order save psychic energy, and how this can involve a degree of complicity between a joker and his audience. The audience's laughter is necessary to validate the joke and sanction the transgression of the taboo. Purdie takes this notion as a starting point for her theory, but revises it in the light of Jacques Lacan's model of the psyche as something which is structured like a language. For Lacan individual identity is created like language as a symbolic system: human subjectivity is made and sustained by language. Language is unstable, however, only having an arbitrary relationship with reality, and its meanings are constantly in flux. As a result the notion of an integrated, coherent self is an illusion: because language is unstable, so the self is unstable. Purdie believes that jokes draw attention to this instability and, in this sense, constitute a different kind of transgression from that suggested by Freud. Jokes flout the rules of language, momentarily shattering the illusion that there is a firm connection between language and the self. Just as broaching a taboo can be a pleasurable thing for the joker and the audience in Freud's scheme, so Purdie's linguistic transgression also has psychological benefits. For Purdie, joking increases the individual's sense of 'mastery' over language, signalling their knowledge of how language signifies; as a result the illusion of psychological coherence is actually strengthened. In short, jokes shatter and simultaneously reinforce the illusion of a stable, coherent self.

Like many of the philosophers we've discussed, Purdie sees incongruity as fundamental to humour, but she also explores its relationship to how we perceive the dislocation between the signifier and the signified (words and the reality they denote). Discussing her reading of jokes, Gillian Pye says that, according to Purdie:

The joker deliberately transgresses the one–to–one relationship of the signifier to the signified that generally governs
signifying processes. He deliberately invokes more than one
'definitionally different' signifier or signified in one semantic
space. In other words he overloads signifying structures and
in so doing draws attention to them. This marking of aberrant
usage, the clear indication that the joker knows he is erring is
[…] absolutely central to the nature of humour. In marking his
error, the joker is effectively asserting his knowledge of the
'correct' procedures of signification, and thereby his identity
as a fully competent 'master of discourse'[63]

According to Purdie, then, jokers assert the possibility of coherent
meaning by deliberately contravening those structures that create the
illusion that meaning is possible. The comic transgression is signalled
as counter to the norm, and in this way jokers disrupt and at the same
time reinforce the illusion of coherence. For Purdie, this is where the
pleasure and psychological benefit of humour is to be found; again
Gillian Pye succinctly summarizes Purdie's ideas:

[the joker] is motivated by the possibility of constructing
control over discursive procedures that are actually unstable.
When the joker transgresses the rules by which unified meaning seems possible, he is simultaneously touching on a fundamental existential anxiety […] By touching on psychological incoherence and the randomness of signifying structures,
however, the joker is able to mark such incoherence as aberrant, as abnormal. This balancing act, in which the possibility of unified meaning is reasserted, may then be conflated
with an (illusory) image of the coherence of self (Gillian Pye,
'Comedy Theory and Postmodernism,' 57).

So jokers disrupt the rules of signification in order to suggest their
power over them; the disruption is implicitly posited as an aberra-
tion—a deviation from the norm—which actually works to strengthen
the norm, implying a stable relationship where there isn't one. In

63 Gillian Pye, 'Comedy Theory and Postmodernism,' *Humor*, 19, 1 (2006) 53–70
(56).

order to illustrate her theory Purdie uses an old joke about Erroll Flynn which I'll paraphrase here:

> Erroll Flynn throws a party and entertains his guests with numerous exotic diversions that keep them captivated throughout the evening. The climax of the night comes when a dwarf musician appears who plays a brilliant rendition of jazz and classical music. Stunned, his guests enquire about the origins of the dwarf instrumentalist. 'I did a favour for a witch a while back,' says Flynn, 'and in return she granted me a wish. Unfortunately she is a bit deaf and she thought I'd asked for a twelve inch pianist.'

The humour is created by a near pun on the word penis, of course, and Freud would interpret it as a tendentious joke that touches on a taboo, saving psychic energy in the process. For Purdie, however, the important thing about the near pun is that it draws attention to the misuse of a signifier: introducing 'penis' alongside 'pianist' highlights the instability of language, and therefore identity; but it also reinforces it because one is forced to replay the rules in order for the joke to work. Purdie's theory is interesting, and to some extent complements traditional theories of humour. Incongruity explains the joke's violation of the relationship between signifier and signified that signals its arbitrary nature; when this is recognised by the joker their view of themselves competent users of language, 'masters of discourse,' is compatible with the notion of superiority too. It also relates interestingly to the fact that humour often deals in taboo and social transgression. As Gillian Pye notes, humour, 'tends to operate at sites of anxiety,' such as those associated with taboos: this suggests a link between using humour to reinforce our sense of a coherent self, and our use of it to address troubling aspects of the world we live in. It is as if humour works to bolster our sense of ourselves as stable individuals at times when our world seems at its least rational and most unstable.

Pause and Reflect.

Consider the way language might work to reinforce social inequities.

Think particularly of gender relations, and the inequalities associated with patriarchy. We have seen how humour can play a reactionary role here, but is there any sense in which it might be employed in a more positive, subversive way?

9.4 The Laugh of the Medusa

The subversive potential of laughter has interested a number of feminist critics associated with postmodernism/poststructuralism. Influenced again by the notion of a fundamental link between language and the psyche, some have looked to humour as a way of subverting the patriarchal language systems we inherit and which colour our thinking. We become social beings when we acquire language, but language is always a reflection of patriarchy. This is important because language is so fundamental to our identity: in a sense language *is* our consciousness, it is *us*, and there is no way of stepping outside it or freeing our thinking from the prejudices it reflects and perpetuates. The language of the social world tends to emphasise structured communication, reason and logic; humour, on the other hand, has affinities with the pre–social and its tolerance of absurdity, play, irrationality, and experimentation. In other words humour often eschews the structures of conventional social discourse, together with its patriarchal values, simplistic oppositions, hierarchies, and ideological prejudices. So one way of evading the latter could be to embrace and exploit the language of humour and play—a medium that might put us in touch with a different kind of experience. In her essay, 'The Laugh of the Medusa' (1975), for instance, Hélène Cixous (1937–) advocates a feminine mode of writing that aims to free itself from the phallocentric discourses of patriarchy; her focus is on the female body and sexuality, but humour and laughter also play a part in her thinking. Her essay alludes to Freud's use of the Medusa myth in his 1922 essay 'Medusa's Head'. Here the Medusa's snake–covered head is used to signify a boy's fear of castration when he first sees an adult female's genitalia (usually his mother's). Later, sight of female genitalia symbolically turns him to stone in the sense that it stiffens his penis in the form of an erection, reminding him that he is not castrated. This is typically phallocentric symbolism, with female genitals symbolizing the absence of something that men possess. The female signifies lack, the obverse of male presence and substance. However, Cixous reclaims the myth by creating a laughing Medusa who refuses the role she has been consigned by patriarchy:

> Too bad for them if they fall apart upon discovering that women aren't men, or that the mother doesn't have one. But isn't this fear convenient for them? Wouldn't the worst be, isn't the worst, in truth, that women aren't castrated, that they have only to stop listening to the Sirens (for the Sirens were men) for history to change its meaning? You only have to look at the Medusa straight on to see her. And she's not deadly. She's beautiful and she's laughing.[64]

Here Cixous reminds us of the patriarchal nature of myth, and the fact that it articulates a falsehood. She does so firstly with reference to the Sirens of Greek mythology: the idea that the Sirens were female temptresses luring men in order to steal their vigour is merely a masculine construction; for Cixous all women must do to free themselves from this, and indeed all male constructions, is to 'stop listening'! As far as Cixous is concerned history is a story that can change its meaning if you actively seek to change it. Crucially this assertion is followed by an image of the laughing Medusa, a myth that Cixous chooses to turn on its head so that the Medusa no longer accepts her role as a signifier of absence: Cixous transforms her into a laughing beauty. The image of the Medusa now becomes a parody of the original myth, a comic inversion that mocks the tradition of exclusion that man–made stories have subjected women to. For Cixous, laughter needs to become part of the language that will free women from the phallocentric narrative dominating history:

> Text: my body–shot through with streams of song; I don't mean the overbearing, clutch 'mother' but, rather, what touches you, the equivoice that affects you, fills your breast with an urge to come to language and launches your force;

---

64 Hélène Cixous, 'The Laugh of the Medusa' trans. Keith Cohen; Paula Cohen, *Signs*, Vol. 1, No. 4. (Summer, 1976), pp. 875–893 (885).

> the rhythm that laughs you; the intimate recipient who makes
> all metaphors possible and desirable; body (body? bodies?),
> no more describable than god, the soul, or the Other; that part
> of you that leaves a space between yourself and urges you to
> inscribe in language your woman's style (Hélène Cixous 'The
> Laugh of the Medusa', 882).

The body will express itself, not through conventional logocentric language, but via 'the rhythm that laughs you.' Humour and laughter are incredibly empowering in Cixous's scheme, then: she uses humour in the form of parody to mock the status quo; she uses laughter to signify the Medusa's defiance, and as a clarion call for all women to deny convention in a similar way; and she positions laughter at the heart of the liberating female narrative of resistance. The laughter is radical because exists outside conventional signifying systems, and it becomes a method of challenging so–called truths, undermining any notion of fixity or stability: women have the potential to 'shatter the framework of institutions [...] blow up the law [...] break up the 'truth' with laughter' (Hélène Cixous 'The Laugh of the Medusa', 888). This sounds quite violent and destructive, but it is also potentially constructive, because it creates a space for new images and ideas, like the image of the laughing Medusa itself.

Creative Writing Exercise

Imagine you are a sculpture of a female nude who has been on display in a museum for the past 100 years. Since you were first sculpted the look on your face has been serene and submissive. Suddenly, however, you feel a wide grin break out across your marble face, and you begin to laugh; as you laugh so you slowly become human, turning from marble to flesh and blood. Try to come up with a plausible cause for the change: it is a response to something funny, but what? Try to make it something that has a bearing on the way the statue feels about its status as a representation of women.

10. Laughter and the Limits of Understanding

For some thinkers associated with postmodernism laughter is symbolic of the limits of meaning, or even the absence of meaning. The French philosopher Jean–Luc Nancy (1940–), for instance, thinks of laughter in a way that reflects Derrida's notion of *Différance*. This view of language implies that meaning is always absent, or infinitely deferred along the chain of signifiers. Words are not in contact with reality—if you look in a dictionary for the meaning of a word you will be referred to another word, and to another word, and so on; original meaning and truth are absent, or present only in traces. This is the view of language associated Deconstruction, a way of analysing texts that focuses on the hierarchical oppositions that underpin meaning. It problematizes the notion of meaning and the view that truth is somehow present or accessible: truths can never be accessed through language; they can only be alluded to. There is no accessible truth, no origin of meaning for thinkers like Jean–Luc Nancy, then, and he feels that laughter can be seen to represent this. In order to make this point he posits what he terms the 'transcendental laugh:'

> What is a transcendental laugh? It is not the obverse of the sign or value accorded to serious matters, which thinking, necessarily reclaims. It is knowledge of a condition of possibility which gives nothing to know. There is nothing comic about it: it is neither nonsense nor irony. This laugh does not laugh *at* anything. It laughs at nothing, for nothing. It signifies nothing, without ever being absurd. It laughs at being the peal of its laughter, we might say. Which is not to say that it is unserious or that it is painless. It is beyond all opposition of serious and non–serious, of pain and pleasure. Or rather, it is at the juncture of these oppositions, at the limit of which they

share and which itself is only the limit of each one of these terms, the limit of their signification.[65]

Here laughter is divorced from the idea of the comic—Nancy's conception of laughter is not about distinctions between 'serious and non–serious,' or oppositions of any kind; rather it reflects the flaw at the heart of all attempts to create meaning; it reflects the ultimate inability of signifying systems to be squared with ultimate meaning. Laughter is, in Andrew Stott's words, a representation of 'a fundamental contradiction that affronts modes of understanding grounded in reason;' it is, 'a kind of metaphysical contradiction encountered at the boundary of reason.' (Andrew Stott, *Comedy*, 143). In short, there is no full meaning for Nancy, and laughter symbolises the point at which this becomes evident.

Simon Critchley also feels that laughter can be an expression of our limitations. When human beings become aware of the limits of understanding, laughter reflects that impasse and returns us to own lowly state: In his book, *Very Little...Almost Nothing: Death, Philosophy, Literature* (1997) he writes:

> Laughter is an acknowledgement of finitude, precisely not a manic affirmation of finitude in the solitary, neurotic laughter of the mountain tops [...] but as an affirmation that finitude cannot be confirmed because it cannot be grasped [...] Laughter returns us to that limited condition of our finitude, the shabby and degenerating state of our upper and lower bodily strata, and it is here that the comic allows with windows to fly open onto our tragic condition (quoted in Andrew Stott, *Comedy*, 142)

This laughter is not a defiant celebration of our shortcomings; rather it functions to remind us of them, forcing us to acknowledge our lowly status and remind us that the human condition is ultimately tragic.

---

65 Quoted in Andrew Stott, *Comedy* (New York: Routledge, 2005) 143.

Pause and Reflect

What is the difference between laughing and smiling? What relationship does smiling have to humour?

Elsewhere Simon Critchley is a little more positive about humour. In *On Humour* (2002) he discusses the smile and its relationship with humour and laughter. For Critchley, the smile is a more modest and appropriate response to the comic nature of the human predicament, more in keeping with its absurdity, and the intractable limitations that we have been discussing. Where laughter has connotations of inappropriate superiority, the smile is more measured and self–effacing:

> Smiling differs from laughter because it lacks the latter's explosiveness. It is silent and subdued. The smile speaks, but not out loud. Its eloquence is reticent [...] a smile is the mark of the eccentricity of the human situation: between beasts and angels, between being and having, between the physical and the metaphysical. We are thoroughly material beings that are unable to be that materiality. Such is the curse of reflection, but such also is the source of our dignity. Humour is the daily bread of our dignity.[66]

The human predicament is a peculiar one: we are physical beings but we are unable to live purely as such. Our self–awareness, which is even more acute in the postmodern world, denies us the bliss of ignorance or instinctiveness. Our capacity for reflection might give our lives dignity, but it also constitutes our curse. As human beings we are caught within a contradiction: the pleasure of knowing is tempered by the pain of not knowing everything, and the smile—given its status as a qualified laugh—is the most apposite expression of this:

> this smile does not bring unhappiness, but rather elevation and liberation, the lucidity of consolation. This is why, melancholy animals that we are, human beings are also the most cheerful. We smile and find ourselves ridiculous. Our wretchedness is our greatness (Simon Critchley, *On Humour*, 111).

66 Simon Critchley, *On Humour* (London: Routledge, 2002) 108–9.

Creative Writing Exercise

> Create a humorous short story that ends with a character laughing;
> then try changing the story so that it closes with the same character
> smiling. How might this alteration influence your reader's response
> to your character, and how the story signifies?

Humour and the Human Predicament

> 'Humour is one of the most serious tools we have for
> dealing with impossible situations.' —Erica Jong.

Simon Critchley feels that humour—in the form of a smile—is an
expression of our humanity; that humour is quintessentially human.
The smile is an acknowledgement of and a consolation for the
human predicament. The English essayist William Hazlitt (1778–
1830) offered a view that chimes well with Critchley's: in 'On Wit
and Humour'(1818) he says, 'Man is the only animal that laughs
and weeps; for he is the only animal that is struck with the difference between what things are, and what they ought to be.'[67] Friedrich
Nietzsche too expresses a similar notion when he says, 'Perhaps I
know best why it is man alone who laughs; he alone suffers so deeply
that he *had* to invent laughter.'[68] In the twentieth century, another
German philosopher, Helmuth Plessner (1892–1985) also argued that
laughter is central to the human experience, and his views are worth
addressing here as we bring the book to a close.

In *Laughing and Crying: A Study of the Limits of Human Behaviour*
(1970), Plessner offers an anthropological view of laughter,
focussing again on the distinction between the mind and the body,
and the difficulty we have integrating the two. For Plessner we are
simultaneously aware of ourselves as mind and body, and the latter,
like the rest of nature, is something that we cannot control, despite
our desire to sustain a coherent sense of self. He suggests that:

> In this respect man is inferior to the animal since the animal

---

67 William Hazlitt, 'On Wit and Humour', *Selected Essays of William Hazlitt 1788–
1830* (Kessinger Publishing, 2004) 410.
68 Friedrich Wilhelm Nietzsche (ed., Reinhold Grimm and Caroline Molina y Vedia)
Philosophical Writings (New York: The German Library, 1995) 241.

does not experience itself as shut off from its physical existence, as an inner self or I, and in consequence does not have
to overcome a breakdown between itself and itself, itself and
its physical existence.[69]

Our awareness of our material nature is forever encroaching on, and
undermining the human ego, creating a contradiction between our
image of self and reality. Laughter and tears are associated with the
moment of that awareness of physical existence. During the act of
either laughing or crying the distinction between body and mind
breaks down: we actually become our bodies; we fall, as it were, from
mind to body. Animals cannot do this because there is nowhere for
them to fall from. When we laugh or cry it is a sign that we are unable
to respond adequately to the world—when we are faced with a conflict that we cannot overcome we are made aware of the fundamental
conflict at the heart of ourselves (the mind/body split); laughter or
tears work to momentarily resolve that conflict by breaking down the
distinction between body and mind. In this sense laughter and tears
are a response to a crisis of human identity. For Plessner, laughter is
more of an intellectual activity than crying, and so involves a greater
degree of disengagement from whatever created the crisis; crying is
usually associated with total emotional immersion. Peter L. Berger
argues that Plessner's view both reinforces the Incongruity Theory of
the comic, and adds an important dimension to it:

Plessner adds the insight that man's eccentricity is the quality that enables him both to perceive the comic and to be an
object of comic perception. Only man belongs to different
levels of being, and this multiple experience of reality is the
basis of comic perception. This is a fundamental anthropological fact that that cannot be reduced to this or that historical
situation. Therefore the comic as such is not a social phenomenon, though of course the contents and occasions of comic
perception vary socially to an enormous degree [...] Put dif-
ferently, what is laughed at and when one might appropri-

69 Helmuth Plessner (transl. by J. S. Churchill & Marjorie Grene) *Laughing and
Crying: A Study of the Limits of Human Behaviour* (Evanston: Northwestern
University Press, 1970) 36.

ately laugh are socially relative, but the underlying incongruity of the comic experience is grounded in an anthropological
reality that transcends all social variations (Peter L. Berger,
Redeeming Laughter, 48).

So for Berger, Plessner's insights help support the view that comic
laughter is not only quintessentially human, but timeless and universal. Despite the fact that what works as comedy can be very culturally
specific, comedy and laughter are transcendent, and stimulated by the
same thing: the perception of incongruity.

Like Critchley, Plessner is interested in the smile, and he sees
smiling not as it's occasionally seen—as a less animated kind of
laughter—but as a different type of response to the comic. As with
Critchley, the difference is one of control: there is a collapse into
bodily awareness with laughter, but this is not the case with smiling;
the smile is more dignified, suggesting an element of mastery over
the situation—mastery, in other words, over the incongruity that for
Plessner parallels the conflict at the heart of the human condition.
In Plessner's words, 'In laughing and weeping man is the victim of
his spirit, in smiling he gives expression to it' (quoted in Peter L.
Berger, *Redeeming Laughter*, 48). Laughter closes the gap between
mind and body, but smiling acknowledges it, and in that moment of
acknowledgement we signal and celebrate our humanity.

Creative Writing Exercise

Imagine you have recently died; at the gates of Heaven the
gatekeeper says: 'In order to gain access you have to explain why
God made humour common to all humankind.' Answer in the form of
a monologue, and try to include as many jokes as possible.

11. Bibliography

11.1 Sources for Traditional Philosophies of Humour and Laughter

Figueroa–Dorrego, Jorge & Larkin–Galiñanes, Cristina., eds., *A Source Book of Literary and Philosophical Writings about Humour and Laughter: The Seventy–Five Essential Texts from Antiquity to Modern Times* (Lampeter: The Edwin Mellen Press, 2009). This huge book contains writing from the majority of important philosophers to have written about humour, but it also goes outside the canon to some extent and presents work by less well–known thinkers, including interesting writers like Demetrius of Alexandria. It breaks into three sections, structuring the material chronologically from antiquity to the Middle Ages, to early-Modern and Modern, each with useful essay–style introductions from the editors. Particularly valuable are those otherwise hard to find texts which offer insights into the relationship between humour, laughter and the Church.

Morreall, John., ed., *The Philosophy of Laughter and Humor* (New York: State University of New York Press, 1987). This is an excellent source of important texts on the philosophy of laughter and humour. It includes key sections from the work of many important thinkers, starting with the ancients and working through to contemporary philosophers: there are extracts from 'traditional theorists' from Plato to Bergson, and a section collecting useful work by modern thinkers like Roger Scruton, Mike W. Martin, and Morreall himself. It also contains a section called 'Amusement and Other Mental States,' which offers material on humour as an emotion, and a section called 'The Ethics of Laughter and Humour,' with work from important humour scholars, Ronald de Sousa and Joseph Boskin. It is true that many of the pre–twentieth century texts are available for free online, but this book conveniently selects the relevant sections, and prefaces them with a summary of how each piece contributes to the various debates about humour and laughter.

11.2 Single Author Works by Modern Philosophers

Berger, Peter L., *Redeeming Laughter: The Comic Dimension of Human Experience* (Berlin: Walter de Gruyter & Co, 1997). Berger approaches humour and laughter from a theological perspective, but his book also offers a good general account of traditional and modern humour theories. It breaks into three sections, the first explores the anatomy of comedy from philosophical, psychological, and social standpoints; the second addresses forms of comic expression including wit, tragicomedy, and satire; the final section presents a theology of the comic. Here he argues that comic incongruity is a feature that unites all forms of humour; drawing among other things on the phenomenon of the Holy Fool, he contends that instances of comic incongruity may imply an incursion of the mystical into the world of reason, and that the divine and the comic may be intimately related. It is an erudite but readable book, offering many useful insights and sensible assessments of existing work on the philosophy of humour.

Cohen, Ted, *Jokes: Philosophical Thoughts on Joking Matters* (Chicago: Chicago University Press, 1999). This short book deals exclusively with jokes, but it covers some valuable ground. It is particularly good on the relationship between jokes and morality, and it includes an excellent section on Jewish humour. It seems to have been written with the popular market in mind, and some of Cohen's points would benefit from more detailed explication, but he is a discerning commentator on the subject and he offers some persuasive critical readings of the various jokes he includes.

Critchley, Simon, *On Humour* (London: Routledge, 2002). Critchley touches on the subject of humour in *Very Little... Almost Nothing* (1997), his book about the question of the meaning of life in a secular world, but *On Humour* is an extended reflection on the role of humour in our lives. It is an eclectic book, referencing a wide range of authors, and he gives his views on several of the key issues of interest to humour scholars, including the question of whether laughter is exclusively human, the ethics of humour, and the relationship between laughter, body and mind. Drawing on the ideas of Plessner, he ends the book with an eloquent celebration of the smile as the quintessential expression of the human condition.

Morreall, John, *A Comprehensive Philosophy of Humor* (Chichester: John Wiley & Sons, 2009). John Morreall is perhaps the best known contemporary philosopher to write extensively about humour. Apart from editing the source book cited above, he has written several noteworthy monographs on the subject, including *Taking Humor Seriously* (1983) and *Comedy, Tragedy and Religion* (1999). He has developed a theory of humour based around incongruity, and he writes about it in an accessible and humorous way. *A Comprehensive Philosophy of Humor* is his most recent book to date, and it includes chapters on the classic theories, the psychology of humour, and the evolution of humour. It presents a succinct overview of the current debates alongside Morreall's personal views on the subject.

11.3 Humour in Cultural and Literary Studies

Jerry Palmer, *Taking Humour Seriously* (London: Routledge, 1994). Palmer offered his own take on the Incongruity Theory of humour in his 1987 book, *The Logic of the Absurd: On Film and Television Comedy,* and *Taking Humour Seriously* develops his interest. Here he examines humour in more depth, drawing on theories from a variety of disciplines including anthropology, psychology, history and sociology. The book contains sections on the occasions for humour, with discussions of joking, clowns and medieval folly; he also has chapters on Freud, gender and humour, and incongruity. His discussion of the latter is particularly comprehensive and useful: it incorporates material from several psychologists working in this field, and Palmer is able to communicate their ideas in a lucid way.

Olsen, Lance, *Circus of the Mind in Motion: Postmodernism and the Comic Vision* (Detroit, MI: Wayne State University Press, 1990). This is a work of literary criticism, but it is one of the first books to include a sustained discussion of the relationship between humour and postmodernism, and it is certainly the most accessible. Olsen offers a theory of postmodern humour which posits comedy as the ultimate subversive force, completely compatible with the postmodern world view. He argues that this force can be creative as well as destructive, and offers a useful antidote to those theorists who can only talk about postmodernism in a negative way.

Sanders, Barry, *Sudden Glory: Laughter as Subversive History* (Boston: Beacon Press, 1995). This is a history of laughter that discusses many of the key philosophical approaches to the subject. It offers particularly informative assessments of Plato, Aristotle and Cicero's readings of laughter, together with discussions of the Freudian and Bahktinian approaches to the topic. Occasionally his ideas can seem a little eccentric—his claim that laughter has its origins in religion, for instance, is not particularly convincing— but nevertheless it is a wide ranging and entertaining book which attempts to offer a complete story of laughter.

Stott, Andrew, *Comedy* (Oxford: Routledge, 2005). This book falls into the category of literary studies and is part of Routledge's New Critical Idiom series offering critical overviews of terms and concepts. Stott spends time discussing philosophies of comedy, and presents lucid explanations of many of the key theories. He is particularly good on Henri Bergson, and includes a succinct Bergsonian reading of Chaplin's *Modern Times* (1936). He also discusses the relationship between comedy and identity, gender, the body, and politics. He has a separate section on laughter which includes an excellent if brief discussion of poststructuralist laughter.

11.4 Books Treating Humour as Philosophy

Hicks, Bill, *Love All the People: Letters, Lyrics, Routines* (London:

Constable, 2004). The stand–up comedian Bill Hicks thought he was a philosopher, and many people have used this term to describe him. You can read this book and judge for yourself. It contains extracts from some of his best known routines, together with other writings. There are entertaining and insightful riffs on religious fundamentalism, abortion, the free press, drug–taking, firearms, and the morality of the first Gulf War. In the piece entitled, 'My Philosophy' he says that he subscribes 'to a philosophy of gentle anarchy' and argues that people are fundamentally virtuous, so much so that if they were left to their own devices, 'a joyful lightness would spread across the face of our dour world.'

Irwin, William., Conard, Mark T., Skoble, Aeon J., eds., *The Simpsons and Philosophy: The D'oh! Of Homer* (Illinois: Carus Publishing Company, 2001). This was the second in a series of books examining how examples of popular culture can become a space for philosophical investigation and debate. This volume has essays from philosophers on subjects such as the Ned Flanders and the idea of neighbourly love, the Simpson family and Kantian morality, and Mr Burns and the notion of happiness. It also includes a list of quotations from fifty philosophers apposite to the show and its preoccupations.

11.5 Humour and Creative Writing

Kachuba, John B., ed., *How to Write Funny: Add Humour to Every Kind of Writing* (Cincinnati: Writers Digest Books, 2001). This is one of the best books for people interested in writing humour. It includes essays on humour writing techniques, some of which are genre specific, covering specialist areas such children's writing, non–fiction, romantic comedy, and even fantasy and science fiction. It also contains some useful interviews with humour writers from a diversity of backgrounds, including Bill Bryson, Sherman Alexie, and Andrei Codrescu.

Rishel, Mary Ann, *Creativity and the Comic Mind* (Detroit, MI: Wayne State University Press, 2002). This book examines the characteristics of humour and discusses a variety of strategies for using humour creatively. Focusing almost exclusively on written humour, it has chapters on, among other things, satire, irony, nonsense, parody, and slapstick. It offers sound, practical advice on the use of comedy writing techniques, and it includes examples from classic humour writers like James Thurber and Woody Allen.

11.6 Online Material

Lippitt, John, Articles on the Philosophy of Humour. John Lippitt is a contemporary English philosopher who has written much worthwhile material on humour. He has written about humour and irony in the work of Kierkegaard, and he also produced a series of articles on humour theory which are available online as PDF files. The latter are particularly useful for students of humour as they offer articulate introductions to the traditional theories, together with Lippitt's own view of their feasibility. Links to his articles on humour and incongruity, humour and superiority, and humour and existentialism can be found below:

https://uhra.herts.ac.uk/dspace/bitstream/2299/3989/1/900211.pdf

https://uhra.herts.ac.uk/dspace/bitstream/2299/3991/1/900210.pdf

https://uhra.herts.ac.uk/dspace/bitstream/2299/3992/1/900208.pdf

Ludovici, Anthony M., *The Secret of Laughter* (1932) Anthony Mario Ludovici (1882–1971) was a British right wing philosopher heavily influence by Friedrich Nietzsche, and this book presents an account of approaches to laughter up to the early twentieth century, together with his own philosophy of laughter. His focus is on laughter as a reflection of superiority, and he endorses Hobbes' view that laughter is an expression of 'sudden glory.' He feels that the modern world goes too far in its celebration of laughter—particularly when related to self–deprecating humour, which he sees as being at odds with human nature. Ludovici's views are extreme and occasionally unsettling, but the book offers an interesting example of a superiority approach to laughter, and students of humour may find his succinct summaries of existing philosophies of laughter illuminating.

http://www.anthonymludovici.com/sl_pre.htm

'Humor and Laughter' This is a site collecting together sections from many important books on humour theory, and includes extracts from Berger, Morreall, and Schaeffer, among others. It is not particularly scholarly in its presentation; the material is not contextualized in any way, and it excludes publication details and even page numbers from the source texts. It offers a useful opportunity to get a flavour of the work of some key theorists, however, and it is recommended for this reason.

https://webspace.utexas.edu/emc597/humor.html#37

The International Society for Humor Studies (ISHS). This is a society dedicated to scholarly humour research. They publish a respected journal, *Humor: International Journal of Humor Research*, and hold regular conferences on humour studies. All serious humour scholars should consider becoming members; membership offers access to the journal, access to scholarly bibliographies, plus discounts on a variety of humour related publications.

http://www.hnu.edu/ishs/

Sources for Jokes. There are numerous sites online that offer access to jokes of various kinds. Most short jokes are not protected by copyright (origin is almost impossible to prove) and people post and share jokes with apparent impunity online. Three of the most popular sites are listed below. All three list jokes in categories. The final link is to Richard Wiseman's LaughLab project which surveyed people in order to discover the world's funniest joke. It includes links to the jokes submitted, and to a report on the project's findings.

http://www.JokesWarehouse.com

http://www.coolfunnyjokes.com/

http://www.101funjokes.com/

http://www.laughlab.co.uk/

Humanities Insights

General Titles

An Introduction to Critical Theory
An Introduction to Rhetorical Terms
Modern Feminist Theory

Genre FictionSightlines

Octavia E Butler: *Xenogenesis / Lilith's Brood*
Reginald Hill: *On Beulah Height*
Ian McDonald: *Chaga / Evolution's Store*
Walter Mosley: *Devil in a Blue Dress*
Tamora Pierce: *The Immortals*

History Insights

Oliver Cromwell
The British Empire: Pomp, Power and Postcolonialism
The Holocaust: Events, Motives, Legacy *
Lenin's Revolution
Methodism and Society
The Risorgimento

Literature Insights

Jane Austen: *Emma*
Conrad: *The Secret Agent*
Dickens: *Bleak House*
Eliot, T S: 'The Love Song of J Alfred Prufrock' and *The Waste Land*
English Renaissance Drama: Theatre and Theatres in Shakespeare's
Time *
William Faulkner: *Go Down, Moses*
William Faulkner: *The Sound and the Fury*
Elizabeth Gaskell, *Mary Barton*
Thomas Hardy: *Tess of the d'Urbervilles*
Joseph Heller: Catch-22 *
G M Hopkins: Selected Poems

Ted Hughes: *New Selected Poems* *
Henrik bsen: *The Doll's House*
D H Lawrence: Selected Short Stories
D H Lawrence: *Sons and Lovers*
D H Lawrence: *Women in Love*
Philip Larkin: Selected Poems *
Paul Scott: *The Raj Quartet*
Shakespeare: *Hamlet* *
Shakespeare: *Henry IV*
Shakespeare: *The Merchant of Venice*
Shakespeare: *Richard II*
Shakespeare: *Richard III*
Shakespeare: *The Tempest*
Shakespeare: *Troilus and Cressida*
Shelley: *Frankenstein* *
Wordsworth: *Lyrical Ballads* *
Fields of Agony: English Poetry and the First World War

Philosophy Insights

Barthes
Thinking Ethically in Business
Critical Thinking and Informal Logic
Existentialism
Formal Logic
Metaethics Explored*
Contemporary Philosophy of Religion*
Plato
Wittgenstein

Also Available from $\mathcal{HEB}$

Jared Curtis, ed.,
*The Poems of William Wordsworth:
Collected Reading Texts from the Cornell Wordsworth.*
3 volumes*

Colin Nicholson, *Fivefathers: Interviews with late Twentieth Century
Scottish Poets*

Keith Sagar, *D. H. Lawrence: Poet* *

* available in paperback

CPSIA information can be obtained at www.ICGtesting.com
Printed in the USA
LVOW07s0148120816

500093LV00001BA/29/P